My Story

Memories of a Martial Art

Grandmaster

By Al Garza Sr.

ISBN: 978-0692428252


Publication rights Sefer Press Publishing House
Questions Comments; SeferPress@israelmail.com

Published by Sefer Press 2015

Cover Design by Al Garza Sr. 2015

Book Format by Al Garza II 2015


Printed in the United States of America 2015

## The Wrath of Tino Tuiolosega

During the 1970's, Douglas Wong and I frequently attended martial arts tournaments in order to enter our students into competition and to act as judges. At one such tournament in Las Vegas at the Convention Center things had not been going well. There were allegations of favoritism, improper judging, and unsportsmanlike conduct, especially by the black belts present. The event had taken a nasty turn in spite of the presence of many well known national and regional champions.

Finally Mr. Tino had had enough. He strode up to the podium snatching the microphone out of the hands of the tournament director. In a loud and threatening voice he addressed the crowd. "My name is Tino Tuiolosega. I think you know who I am. All of you so called black belts are a disgrace. All of the cheating and poor sportsmanship at this tournament is disgusting. If any of you don't like what I'm saying then step up and fight me right here, right now. One at a time or all at once, I don't care! Who's first!"

The audience was stunned into silence, not a soul moved or dared to say a word as real fear spread throughout the room. Mr. Tino was famous for his unparalleled fighting skills and well known as a strict disciplinarian who was not adverse to meting out instant punishment to anyone who stood in his way.

After a few moments of uncomfortable silence, Mr. Tino warned the entire tournament that if things didn't change he'd return and people would get hurt! He then threw down the mic and stormed off the stage with a stern look on his face. As he approached Doug and me, he glanced at us and with his back to the crowd he smiled and winked at us. We all cracked up laughing while the rest of the auditorium was practically shivering in terror. Another reminder that Mr. Tino was not to be crossed by anyone and would not stand for misconduct.

Prof. Carl Totton

# TABLE OF CONTENTS

# Introduction

Memories of a Grandmaster are based on a true story about Al Garza, as a young man who tells his story about his experiences and friendship with his martial arts Grandmaster Tino Tuiolosega. This book recounts his many journeys with Grandmaster Tino and chronicles of the early history of GM Tino and his Polynesian art of self-defense Lima Lama, "The Hands of Wisdom."

## My Source of References
Throughout Tino's career I have also been honored and blessed to be the only one allowed to film and videotape him during his demonstrations. My personal experiences and vast film library contains interviews with: his first wife Claire; his first five students; and the original Lima Lama organizational board members. Much of my book recounts not only comes from my early experiences but also from my interviews that are video recorded.

**Lima Lama Master Teacher**
**Al Garza**

# Acknowledgement

**Story Written By – Al Garza**

**Content Consultant – A. Falcon Entertainment Company**

**First Editor – Dave Cater**

**Assistant in Prof-reading – Denise Heady, Aram Sanchez**

**And May Garza**

**Second Editor and Book Set-up – Al Garza II**

# My Story
## Memories of A Martial Art
## Grandmaster

# Dedication

This book is dedicated to the entire Lima Lama practitioners. It was written so all Lima Lama practitioners may have a common understanding of their Lima Lama's early history and its founder Grandmaster Tino Tuiolosega.

## Author Al Garza

# About the Author

I was nine in 1954 when my father brought us to Los Angeles from my native San Antonio, Texas. Five of us (I was the oldest of three children) shared a small, two-bedroom house in East Los Angeles. Our family would eventually grow to include seven children, five of whom are girls. I received my early self-defense training from my father, Alfred Garza, who boxed as a featherweight while also toiling as a printer. My dad gave me my first self-defense lesson. I loved boxing from the first punch and it awakened in me a fascination for hand-to-hand combat.

That fascination turned into downright passion thanks to Hollywood and the exploits of James Bond. In the 1964 thriller *Goldfinger*, Sean Connery's character is pitted against "Oddjob", played by real-life judo master Harold Sakata. This picture forever changed my life. It had an extravagant music score, an interesting plot, picturesque locations and elegant women. But what attracted me most were the karate and judo fighting that featured real-life hand-to-hand combat sequences. (The world was later introduced to the art of Ninjutsu in the 1967 Bond pic, *You Only Live Twice*).

I realized I had a passion for Asian martial arts and Asian culture. It was inevitable that I would become involved in martial arts. I found a Judo school and life as I knew it was over. What lay ahead was a career as a martial arts teacher, television and video producer, and finally historian. After decades of hard work and experimentation, as well thousands of hours of study with some of our generation's great masters, I created my own hand-to-hand combative teaching system.

**Grandmaster Tino Tuiolosega**

This book not only chronicles my early martial arts journey, but more importantly honors the person who inspired me as a student and treated me as a member of his family. This man was Tino (Tino Tuiolosega), better known as "Mr. Lima Lama" (*Hands of Wisdom*). After reaching Grandmaster levels in several styles of Kung-fu and Kenpo Karate, Tino created "Lima Lama," a highly sophisticated and deadly fighting system that showed respect and admiration for his American/Polynesian heritage.

The beginning of this treatise reveals the history of Lima Lama based upon my lifelong relationship with teacher and close friend, Grandmaster Tino Tuiolosega; my interaction with the Tuiolosega family; Mr. Tino's original students; and other dedicated students and masters of the art.

**Tino Tuiolosega—The Early Years**

Tino Tuiolosega was commonly known as a street fighter in his native Samoa before discovering the joys of boxing during a stint in the U.S. Marines. In the early 1960s, he met the legendary Ed Parker and began studying the Chinese/Hawaiian martial art of Kenpo Karate. Tino immediately took to the training and rose like a Phoenix through the ranks. In fact, he was entrusted with teaching Parker's Black Belts—even though he was still a *brown belt*.

Although he soon received his Black Belt in Kenpo Karate, Tino was far from satisfied. While Tino was studying Kenpo Karate with Ed Parker, he met Grandmaster Ark Wong, who in 1963 became the first Chinese instructor to teach kung-fu to *gwei-los (non-chinese)*. Grandmaster Wong opened his first school in the Chinatown section of Los Angeles. This small section of the Chinese community was inaugurated in 1938, although in reality Chinese immigrants had lived there since 1870. Ultimately, Tino accomplished the extraordinary: he earned Grandmaster titles in five kung-fu styles and garnered the distinction of becoming one of the few non-Chinese to breathe such rarified martial arts air. Unsurprisingly, Tino formed his Lima Lama organization in the mid 1960s with five American martial artists. To his organization he later added Rigor Lopez, a martial artist of Mexican descent. Mexico today boasts the largest population of Lima Lama practitioners in the world, with more than 50,000 under its banner.

**The Origin of Lima Lama**

Grandmaster (GM) Tino Tuiolosega defined Lima Lama (Lima Lama) as "the Hands of Wisdom" and stressed that his Lima Lama was never a Polynesian martial art by culture or tradition (as some have interpreted to be). Instead, GM Tino classified his art as American Samoan because of his heritage. Lima Lama's development is derived solely from GM Tino; no one else can rightly lay claim to this distinction. Although many have contributed to the growth of the art, only GM Tino is responsible for its creation. Holding to the law of cause and effect, the Lima Lama style and organization were born, after which a board of directors was formed.

## Born in Tutuila (Pago Pago), American Samoa

Tino was an only child. His father, Tuumamao Tuiolosega, and mother, Sapo Alugo, were originally from the Island of Olosega and Sapsapoaluga Feagaimaleata Poumele Tuiolosega, which lies about 45 minutes by plane from Pago Pago and boasts a small population of about 300. The name Tui means "King" and olosega means island. Now, don't be confused by the term "King." Unlike most Western cultures where "King" is associated with a wealthy monarchy, the proper title for Mr. Tuiolosega Sr. is High Chief—a moniker bestowed by virtue of the island or islands he owned. Tino's grandfather was titled "King" but later the government abolished such titiles and changed it to High Chief.

The Samoan culture is a Clan community, meaning the oldest male of the family is given much respect and control over family matters. Even though Tino was the only birth child, he was never without a brother or sister. The Tuiolosega's would often adopt children and raise them as their own. Since they carried the Tuiolosega name, Tino knew them simply as brothers and sisters. The family later moved to the island Tutuila and lived in the harbor village called Pago Pago where Mr. Tuiolosega Sr. was a well-respected court judge. Tino was raised a strict Christian and came from a church-going family. His parents were very loving to their only son, but they also tried to instill discipline into his life.

**Court Judge Mr. Tuiolosega Sr.**

It was during one of my many trips with Tino and his family that I visited American Samoa. A local tour of the town took us inside the courthouse, where we saw Mr. Tuiolosega's picture (Tino's dad) hanging with all the other judges. I recorded Tino standing next to the picture of his father, his fingers first touching his lips and then lovingly placing them on his father's image as he was giving him the son to father respect. It was an emotional moment as tears fell from Tino's eyes.

# Chapter 1
## The Arena Mexico 2000

*Sitting in a rustic room, the master patiently waits for his appearance to be announced. He is scheduled to give a demonstration for the large audience at an historical sports arena in Mexico. He tries to relax by breathing slowly and deeply. At the same time, he anticipates the moment he steps before the audience.*

*This middle-aged man with salt and pepper hair may be small in stature, but he looms large in his crisp, black martial arts uniform. He knows the responsibility he shoulders when performing Lima Lama to his peers. He searches for a state of complete stillness that will help him achieve the concentration needed for his demonstration. Thousands of spectators in the arena show their excitement for the demonstration about to begin. Their voices grow louder and more pronounced as they scurry through the tunnel and into their seats.*

This was truly an exciting moment for the revered city of Acapulco, Mexico, because it marked the first Master's Black Belt sport-fighting tournament organized by the Lima Lama Mexican Federation. This annual national competition determines the 10 Black Belt Lima Lama Tournament fighters who will represent Mexico at the international championship in Spain, Hawaii and other countries. This competition is exclusively for Black Belts to ensure that Lima Lama can be represented at the highest level in Mexico.

Amazingly, the organization has become the largest martial arts collective in Mexico! And as a special treat to the audience, the master will be demonstrating his own style of Lima Lama. What you can expect from the Federation of Mexico, Lima Lama is one of the best of the martial arts.

*Moments later the Master hears his name. He approaches a full mirror near a gray stonewall and gazes at his reflection. This stirs memories in the Master of another time. He reminisces about a place and time when he was not alone, when he was sitting in front of his martial arts Master. The place: Brea, CA. The time: 1968.*

# Chapter 2
## Official Student in Lima Lama

**Diamond Bar, CA**

It was 1968 and I was young, inspired, excited, but nervous as I waited inside the living room of the gentleman I hoped would become my next martial arts teacher. I was here to see if I would be accepted as his new student. However, I knew he would only accept me under certain conditions. When it came accepting a new student, Tino Tuiolosega took the task very seriously. Here I was, sitting in front of this mammoth, 6-foot-2, intimidating-looking Samoan martial artist, a Grandmaster that was well known and feared in the martial arts community. He was known simply as Mr. Tino. He was considered a no-nonsense individual who would challenge anyone anytime, regardless of size or combat experience.

Tino is a Polynesian Samoan who sported the physique of a chiseled middleweight boxer. His eyes were deep set and intimidating. One glance would stir fear into any man. This proud Samoan's grandfather was considered the King in the Pacific Island of Olosega while his father was a High Chief.

*"Now I am in the presence of a respected and great martial artist,"* I said to myself.

Tino is the Grandmaster and founder of the martial art style: Lima Lama, meaning *"Hands of Wisdom"* in the Samoan language. I was here solely to be accepted as his "*official*" student. He sat in front of me, staring. After what seemed an eternity, he finally spoke, "*Are you a spy?*"

I was stunned and puzzled by the question because by then I had known him for over two years. As Tiny Lefiti's first Black Belt student, I had been to Tino's home (with Tiny for lessons) a number of times. I looked at him and said, "*No! Of course, not.*"

Tino continued: "*Did Guzman send you here to steal my art?*" (Dan Guzman was my first Karate teacher)

"*No,*" I insisted. "*Nobody sent me here! I just want to learn from you. I came to be accepted as your student, that's all.*"

He leaned forward, pushed his shoulders upward, and glaringly said, "*I don't like people to cross me, understand?*"

"*I wouldn't,*" I confirmed.

"*OK,*" he responded, "*I'll accept you as my exclusive student.*"

That moment forever altered my life. I was finally and officially his "exclusive" student. Our first lesson included the inward block, a hand block with a vertical central alignment. At the end of my lesson, he pointed for me to sit on the floor.

"*Let me show you something,*" he said. He walked into another room and came back with a large certificate with his picture on the right-hand corner.

"*This is my Kung-Fu Grandmaster's diploma, given to me by five Chinese Grandmasters. Each one taught me their style of Kung-Fu and I'm the only non-Chinese person who ever received this title with five different Grandmaster's signatures. In return, I promised them that I would accept a Grandmaster's position in their Chinese association of Kung-Fu. They want me to teach Kung-Fu to their members.*"

"*Are you?*" I asked.

"*No,*" he replied. "*I decided to go on my own and start my own style of martial art. I don't need them. I don't need anybody. I'll tell you what gets me mad (and that is) when some people start calling my art Kenpo style. Just because I'm also a Grandmaster of the Kenpo system doesn't mean I'm teaching it. I told this Kenpo guy that if I ever hear him call my art Kenpo I would ring his neck.*"

I later discovered that Tino was angry over what people were saying about his newly created Lima Lama martial art. Those who were critical of him, however, could not conceive what Tino had invented. These people lacked the expertise, education, or the talent to understand what Tino had created. This new and revolutionary fighting style of Lima Lama was far beyond their comprehension. To reach this level and create Lima Lama was an extraordinary achievement for Tino, but much of the martial arts population was narrow-minded in their views. They could not see the man's brilliance, even when it was right in front of them. Tino was frustrated, because he could not understand why others were so critical. Moreover, he was less forgiving of people who disrespected his Lima Lama. Only those who witnessed Lima Lama first hand knew of its awesome capabilities. This was especially true of those who sparred with him or assisted him in his demonstrations of Lima Lama's speed and power. With Tino, seeing was believing. Anyone who witnessed him in action immediately recognized his greatness. Clearly, he was one of the most-feared fighters of his generation. If someone showed disrespect, he had no problem taking the necessary action to remedy the situation. Tino's background spoke for itself.

He trained in Chinese Kenpo Karate and earned a high Black Belt from one of the largest Kenpo Karate organizations in the United States. He possessed the title of Grandmaster in five styles of Kung-Fu; excelled as a boxer; and earned a reputation as a tough-as-nails street fighter in Hawaii. This impressive resume of form and function made Tino a fighter among fighters, a man feared for his technique and respected for his skill. Still, the Kenpo situation upset him.

*"Watch this,"* he said, picking up the phone and dialing a number.

*"Hello, how are you?"* He listened for a minute and then suddenly raised his voice to the person on the other side of the phone. *"Let me tell you why I'm calling you. I heard that you said Lima Lama came from your group. That everything I know came from your martial art culture. If you're saying this I am going to break your neck, understand?"*

He gives me the phone so I can listen to the voice on the other phone.

*"I didn't say that, you know I wouldn't say anything like that."* the man responded. *"You're like a brother to me."* Tino took the phone from me and spoke again.

*"I better not hear any more things about you saying anything about me, or about Lima lama. Good-bye."* With that he slammed down the phone and said, *"See I told you he's afraid of me. I'll break him if he talks bad about me."*

Tino continued, *"You know Al, You have to put your life on the line if you're going to be a leader. You have to put fear in them. Fear is a strong emotion. That's how you control people; you make them be fearful of you."*

I was both stunned and awestruck. It was a moment I would remember forever.

# Chapter 3
## Fear to Gentleness

## Back in Acapulco, Mexico

*In that room at the Lima Lama Tournament in Mexico, the master remains deep in thought. He imagines his teacher. Tino instilled so much fear in people.*

*This need to instill fear in others may have derived from the insecurity that Tino experienced in his childhood upbringing in Pago Pago.*

## Reflecting on His Past

The early 1960s found Tino in the formative stages of creating his Lima Lama style. From the start, the public was less than receptive. In fact, people laughed at his new art. It was not common practice for a person to simply proclaim the creation of a new martial arts style. After all, the Chinese had already created hundreds of martial arts styles over thousands of years. The newer the style, the less credence it was afforded by the martial arts community. "How can someone dare to create a new martial art? And someone so young at that?" (they seemed to be saying). It was well known that Tino Tuiolosega needed the respect of others, especially with those who doubted his prowess as a fighter and creator of Lima Lama. It was during this time that Tino found that the quickest route to respectability was through fear.

At Ed Parker's Long Beach Internationals one year, I saw Tino point and then poke a World Karate Grand Champion in the chest. I mean, he was in his face! It appeared that Tino was trying to intimidate the champion. This escalated to the point where Tino challenged this champion to a fight—right there and then. Talk about tension. That Karate champion was in shock, a look of terror on his face. He stood there motionless as Tino continued with the verbal assault. Tino then turned and walked away; leaving a champion who looked like someone had just stolen his trophy. He was crushed. I never asked Tino about this incident and Tino never explained his actions. Reflecting on the incident, I was just as shocked as everyone else.

However, nothing remains the same. Life always changes and Tino was no exception. Tino grew wiser and his actions became more controlled. In his later years, the "fear philosophy" he leaned on for strength and control gave way to a gentler and kinder demeanor. He learned that a better way to earn respect was through kindness and respect toward others. As a natural response, people would manifest and offer him the respect and admiration he so much treasured. He incorporated this new philosophy into the very fabric of his Lima Lama teachings. Like all great martial arts, Lima Lama was growing and evolving.

# Grand Master Tino Tuiolosega 1966

*Tino in his early 30's*

*Grandmaster Tino Tuiolosega and Al Garza (1968)*

*As the master waits for his turn in front of a packed arena audience, he thinks to himself: "Those days seem so far away, and now look how far this art has come. I have traveled to so many countries teaching Lima Lama, even far more than I could have ever imagined."*

# Chapter 4
## The Death Touch "Dim Mok" Part 1

### 1968 Diamond Bar, CA

The Master is sitting inside his room when he hears a strange sound behind the sofa. The Master investigates and finds a 10-year-old boy.

*"Little boy, what are you doing on the floor behind the sofa?"*

The Master then bends forward, picks up the little boy and places him on the sofa.

*"What are you doing hiding there?"* The Master repeats.

*"Nothing Master. I just wanted to see what you looked like and talk to you. I'm a blue belt in Lima Lama."*

*"Ah, a blue belt,"* The Master says. *"That's very promising. You are almost a master. Very good, what's your name?"*

*"I am called Louis,"* The boy responds. The boy is nervous, but excited to have this chance with the Master.

*"Please Master; I want to ask you questions."*

*"What questions do you have little boy."*

*"I have heard so many tales about you and your teacher. I want to know if they are all true and I also want to know more stories,"* The boy relates.

*"My, you are a curious one,"* The Master tells him. *"But since you're here keeping me company I'm going to tell you a story about my GM Master Tino and myself. After all, it's just you and myself here so let's be friends."* The Master shakes the boy's hand as if it were the hand of someone he had known for a long time.

*"Good. My name is Master Al Garza. Now that we have introduced each other formally, I'll tell you something about myself and then later you can share with me something about yourself. So what is your first question little boy?"*

*"I have heard that you can hurt a man or even kill with a single touch. Is that true master?"*

The Master looks at the little boy. *"You have heard that, really? I didn't know such stories were told of me. I'll tell you what I know about Dim Mok, so you can understand a little about it. I'll start with my story about the secret of Tino's Death Touch, Dim Mok."*

The boy smiles and his eyes widen with anticipation. The Master sees genuine interest and he is pleased.

## A Story About His Past

I remember waiting for Tino in his living room. He had a medium-sized three-bedroom house in Diamond Bar, CA. When his son Nelson, Buzzy as we called him, greeted me, he sported red and black bruises on his arms and neck.

*"What happened to you? Why are you all bruised up?"* I asked.

He just smiled and explained that he was sparring with the guys in the garage. The garage was Ground Zero for all Lima Lama training. Capable of accommodating two cars, it was empty excluding a punching bag and some weights hugging the base of the walls.

*"It got kind of rough with the guys, but it was fun,"* Buzzy said and added. *"I got to go Al. I got a date with my girlfriend. I'll see you later."* With that, Buzzy was gone.

Waiting for Tino was a common occurrence, especially since he worked the night shift as a supervisor at a manufacturing company. His martial art teaching schedule suffered if he had to work overtime. When this was the case and Tino was catching up on his sleep, Tino's wife, Claire, their eldest daughter Cookie or Tino's stepsister Taumaloto, would keep me company. Claire was always respectful, with good moral principles. Sometimes we would sit at the kitchen table and she would tell me stories about how she met Tino; how Tino was raised in Samoa; or why he left Samoa to go to

Hawaii. She also liked to relate how they met and how she fell in love with him when he was still in the Marine Corps.

Cookie was the eldest of seven children and was only 16 years of age. Taumaloto was Tino's adopted sister and was 17 years of age. She also originated from Samoa. Both Cookie and Taumaloto were amiable and sensitive, respectful girls. In fact, everyone in the Tuiolosega family treated me with kindness and respect. Cookie and Taumaloto were always taking care of the younger brothers and sister. Taumaloto would also clean the house and cook for the family. Unfortunately, because of her age, she wasn't allowed to date nor have friends outside the family. However, I had the blessing of developing a good, sincere and respectable friendship with her. Tired of the grind, she ran away a few years later and got married. When we reconnected she had six children and was living in Rosemead, CA. I visited her often after that. One day when I went to her home her real sister from Samoa told me that Taumaloto had died the previous week of a recently discovered brain tumor. Losing such a good friend rendered me speechless. Taumaloto was a good person with a good soul. I will always remember her with the utmost respect and hold her memory close to my heart.

One of my fondest memories was seeing the girls scatter when Tino would finally wake up. They weren't allowed to talk to me when Tino wasn't present. Today, I laugh every day I remember how the sisters panicked when they heard their father's footsteps. If Tino had discovered them simply talking to me, he would have disciplined them. I recall one afternoon when Tino came into the living room searching for his son.

"*Where's Buzzy*? He inquired.

"*I told that kid he couldn't leave the house.*" Tino was angry. "*You see Al, these kids can drive you crazy.*"

He explained that he had disciplined him time and time again, but that Buzzy ignored his wishes. Claire then expressed her concern.

"*Tino, you're too tough with the kids. Just like last night you were so rough with the guys.*" Tino looked at me and smiled.

I looked at him and said, "*So it's true what Tiny and the guys told me about the finger sets?*"

Again, he smiled and then shared the training session. "*You should have seen the workout I had with the guys.*"

Tino re-enacted the incident, replete with hand gestures, finger pointing and body movements. He added that his instruction included Chinese pressure point death touch hits.

"*They just looked at each other and kind of smirked at me, in disbelief,*" Tino said with wry amusement. "*So I said, 'OK, line up, one at a time and punch at me!' When I said that, they just looked at each other kind of scared, cause they knew I was upset with them for smirking at me. They also knew I meant business when I said punch at me. They had no choice but to follow my orders or else.*

*Then they lined up, Al, and one at time they came at me. First came Sal—he tried to hit me with a strong body punch to my chest, Bam. I hit him in his arm and ribs. Down he went, out cold."*

Now Tino was smiling.

*"Next came Richard. He's the smart one. Every time he would punch at me, it was from far away. This way, he was able to start running backward after his punch. He wouldn't even come close to me. He didn't want me to hit him. I felt bad and did not continue with my counterattack. I just let him go without getting hurt. Then I said, 'Tiny you're next', Tiny came with everything he had, with all his 250 pounds. This big guy tried to hit me in the head but 'Pow!' I uppercutted him in the stomach and lifted him up about six inches off the ground. He was out for the day. I knocked him out cold. 'John, you're next.' I pointed to him, 'John, come on! Attack me!' John slowly moved at me and I tell you Al, he looked white and pale. I mean he was scared standing there. I told him 'shoot', and he did. He shot a right-hand cross to my face. I blocked it and then hit him solid to the right side of his neck. And then I hit him in the chest. He must have bounced back about five feet. After I hit him, the guy really scared me. I thought I killed him; he was shaking and white foam was coming out of his mouth. I was worried. I turned him over and started to rub his back and place wet towels on his forehead.*

*That's when I quit hitting the guys and gave them a break."*

*"See Tino,"* Claire interjected, *"I told you before, some day you're going to kill somebody. You have no control when you teach and you're always hurting someone."*

The Master is back in the stadium talking to Louis.

> *"You see Louis, during those early years of my training with GM Tino, his wife Claire was the inside information source to Tino's life. She was there as the eyewitness to Tino's personal training. Claire was the person I trusted when it came to Tino's stories. I knew she would tell me the truth without exaggerating."*

This characteristic would help me weed out fact from fiction when it came to Tino's stories. It was simple: Claire would discretely glance at me after Tino had said something unusual or what seemed like an exaggeration. When Tino wasn't looking, I would turn toward Claire and she would either nod to confirm something happened or shake her head to signify the story was an exaggeration. However, there was no denying what I saw, what I heard from other students, or what I felt when Tino was teaching me or demonstrating a movement. His Lima Lama was extremely powerful and potentially lethal.

**1967 Tino demonstrating finger technique to eye**

# Chapter 5
## "Dim Mok", Part II

### The Finger Set Of Lima Lama

The Dim Mok story was confirmed by Tino's wife, but I knew I wanted to, or more importantly, needed to know more. The boy asks the master: *"Oh please tell me more."*

*"As I was telling you earlier, I was very curious about what happened that Friday evening and very interested on how Tino had applied his Dim Mok (he called it the finger set techniques). After what Tino had told me about the Dim Mok incident, I decided to investigate this event to obtain more answers on what occurred that evening. My plan was to question Tiny, Richard, Sal, John, and Solomon. During that time, I was training with Tiny Lefiti and also going twice a week to Tino Tuiolosega's house to train with him. One Monday evening while I was teaching a Lima Lama class for Tiny, I noticed he entered the school and headed straight for his office. Something was different; he was walking as though he was ill or injured. After my class, I went to Tiny's back office to see if he was OK. Tiny was sitting in his chair. As I entered, he stared at me with a strange look and told me,*

*"Al, you are not going to believe me when I tell you what happened last Friday at Tino's home. Man, it was something else."*

*"What happened?"* I asked.

"*You know how Tino would always mention to us about his Dim Mok death touch strike and how we always say 'ya right' and joke about it?* Tiny asked rhetorically. "*Well, this last Friday he got so upset with us that he told us to attack him one at a time. It was something else. First, he told Sal to throw a karate punch at his face. After he blocked Sal's right hand, Tino hit him twice, once to his right arm and then to the right side of his body. Sal went backward, hit the garage wall and started to vomit on the side of the garage. Richard then moved away from Tino, looking scared and saying,*

*'No way man, I'm not punching at you. I'm not crazy.'*

*Solomon just looked at Richard and said, 'Me neither, not me.' Then Tino pointed to me to attack him or else…you know how he gets when he has that look on his face. I nodded at Tino as a response to his command and punched him with a strong right hook. The next thing I knew I was looking up from the floor and seeing stars. Al, I don't know what hit me. My eyes were open but my mind was not there; I couldn't move my body. Then he told John to attack him and the next thing you know, POW! Tino hit him on his left rib. John hit the floor and started shaking. We got worried about him. Then Tino walked to John and started to massage his back to bring him back from his almost-unconscious state. After a few minutes, John was all right and I started to get my feeling back. Sal wasn't feeling well and he was really red and swollen in the arm and body. Tino also had to massage his body and arm. I don't know what he did, but I'm telling you, we are not going to joke about his finger sets or Dim Mok anymore."*

I asked Tiny if he had seen how Tino had hit each of them.

*"No,"* Tiny replied, *"Tino moved too fast to see his hands or his fingers. I was only thinking about the pain that I had."*

Tiny then lifted his shirt to show me a dark bruise on his stomach. I immediately noticed a corrugated bruise that was red and black and about six inches in diameter. A few days later I went to see Sal at his school and told him what I had heard from Tiny. Sal said nothing; he just smiled and pulled back the sleeve of his shirt to show me his right arm. He also had a bruise, but it was black and blue from biceps to shoulder. He then lifted his shirt and I saw one-half of his right upper body was equally battered and discolored. It looked like he'd been clobbered with a baseball bat.

Next on the list was Richard Nunez. Since Richard watched Tino hit everyone else, I thought he might offer a different perspective. I told him I had seen Tiny and Sal's bruises. Richard shook his head and said,

*"It's true. I was next to Tino when he got angry at everybody and threatened us to either punch at him or else. When it was my turn, I punched him then ran back so he couldn't catch me."*

"*Did you see him how he hit the other guys? Did you see any of the finger techniques?*" I asked.

"*Not really,*" he admitted. "*Tino was too fast and I was worried after Tiny got knocked out. I just lost my concentration and could only think about what kind of damage Tino could do to me.*"

I realized there and then I wasn't going to get any answers about Dim Mok from the guys. So I waited until I saw Tino again to ask him myself. The next evening I went to Tino's home. When I arrived, he was still asleep so I waited in the living room with Claire. I detailed everything that Tiny and the other guys had shared about the Friday night incident. Claire listened attentively and then told me that before the class started, Tino was already upset because every time he mentioned the finger sets to the guys they would make jokes about the topic.

He told her that he was going to teach them a lesson that evening. Claire's story was identical to Tiny's. As Claire finished her story, Tino walked in and sat on his chair next to me.

"*It's true what she's telling you,*" he admitted. "*I was very upset with them and that's why I did that to them.*"

Back at the Stadium, the boy is wide-eyed and speechless as the Master finishes his story. The boy implores the Master to keep going.

*"Wow, what an incredible story. Master tell me more."*

The Master lifts the boy from the sofa and tells him return to his parents, because they might be worried about him.

*"Go back to you parents and come back later."* The boy agrees.

*"Yes Master, I'll come back. I'm so excited to have met you. Thank you very much."* As the boy wave's good-bye, the Master once again reflects on the Dim Mok story.

**Tino's home in Diamond Bar California**

Tino mentioned Dim Mok was a two-part application: one part involved the striking method; the other part took into consideration the application of the technique. He said he hesitated showing it to me, because it was just too dangerous and with knowledge came great responsibility. Years later, when we were in the hospital after Tino's first heart attack, he reminded me about what he had said about the finger set.

Much to my surprise, I started my lessons on the finger sets that day. My study included finger exercises, executions, angles, combinations, theories and pressure point positions. I believe he did this because he actually thought he would die at the hospital.

**Grandmaster Tino Tuiolosega (1998)**

# Chapter 6
## Diverse Students

### Back in the Stadium

*The Master stares at the solitary figure in the mirror and reminisces about his days with Tino's Lima Lama.*

Tino taught mostly expert Black Belt practitioners. He only had a few students with a limited martial arts background. It was quite obvious by the students he selected that there was urgency in Tino's agenda, almost as though he could sense time was running out. He believed he had to teach his Black Belt students Lima Lama as soon as possible to expand his Lima Lama organization. Another reason for choosing experienced martial artists was the advanced nature of the teaching. He taught complex self-defense movements consisting of three or more continuous steps. They were quite different from anything his students had seen. Each student had to quickly adjust as the techniques changed from week to week. This teaching method was what one would call a "crash course" in advanced learning. Most martial arts styles feature the standard block and strike technique. Lima Lama, or "the Hand of Wisdom" was unique in approach and function. The motions appeared beautiful and flowing, but behind the almost-hypnotic exterior was a brutality of deadly proportions. Only those who showed true loyalty and faithfulness to the art were shown its potent techniques.

# Chapter 7
## Training Sessions With Tino

It was good that I was young and driven. The techniques Tino taught me had to be practiced over and over. I even worked the changes Tino made to each movement. I admit that the continuous alterations were a source of frustration to other students. While their frustration may have been justifiable, I regarded them as positive, because I saw how the moves could be adapted to different combat situations. Practicing this way proved to be a blessing in disguise. I not only discovered new ways of applying movements, but it also opened up my way of thinking about how things fit together.

I'd visit Tino's house two or three times a week for lessons. I was progressing at a fast pace, because I was working hard on my off days. My lessons took place usually around 10 a.m. If Tino had stayed up late the night before, I would wait patiently until he walked in the living room or the kitchen. The lessons would last about two-to-three hours. When someone else would stop by we might end up having a group class. During my private lessons, Tino would show me a technique and then add variations on that technique. When I returned for the next lesson, he would show me another technique and then improvise again. It was a mountain of information to see and learn, but I loved it. It was challenging and fun on one hand, but deadly serious on the other hand. It was Lima Lama and I was up for the challenge.

As soon I got home from a lesson, I ate a light dinner and then went right back to work. Many students grew frustrated with the constant changes. But my mind was like a sponge soaking up every piece of information I could get my hands on. New moves plus new techniques equaled new challenges on a daily basis. It was quite clear to me now what drove me to want more. One factor was my personal character. But it was also my personal mission to incorporate Lima Lama into every part of my being. I wanted to live it, breathe it, and feel it in my bones. The more time we spent together, the more Tino felt about sharing his experiences in martial arts, his relationship with Ed Parker, Kung-Fu teachers, the training and his plan for Lima Lama. I was always attentive, genuinely respectful, and made sure I validated Tino's trust in me. I know that he recognized my effort and the value I placed in his art. In time, the Grandmaster-teacher-student friendship matured. This trust allowed Tino to be comfortable enough talk with me about his personal aspirations or sensitive family matters. Thanks to our unique interaction, I eventually learned why he made so many changes to his techniques.

*"I intentionally taught that way because I wanted to test the loyalty, patience and intention of each student of mine before I teach them the pure Lima Lama,"* Tino told me. *"I know that at times I would confuse and frustrate them but that was part of my plan."*

My suspicions were correct. Also I thought he might be using his students as guinea pigs to practice what he had developed and created. It also served to test Lima Lama's effectiveness in a variety of situations.

Later that evening we talked about his upbringing in Samoa. For the first time I could sense Tino was comfortable sharing his innermost feelings. He began to share his family heritage.

*"Wait here, I'm going to show you something I've never shown to anyone outside the family,"* Tino said, getting up from his chair.

Tino came back with a book. He placed the book on the living room table and said,

*"See this Al. It's my family tree from Samoa…my lineage."*

Tino opened the book and I saw names recorded on the page from top to bottom. He pointed to each name and explained the positions they held in the Island of Olosega. It was amazing to see his ancestry written down. As I looked at his ancestry book I could see the title of High Chief went back many lifetimes. I could only imagine what it was like being a High Chief in Samoa a century ago.

# Tutuila Island

# 1996 Pago Pago Picture from Al Garza

**America Samoa, Pago Pago picture by Al Garza**

# Chapter 8
## Friday Nights Members Only

I was at Tino's home at least three times a week, mostly in the evening. To get as much training time as possible, I had to accommodate his schedule. I planned my whole day around practicing Lima Lama. I really looked forward to the weekends, because I could practice without the typical daily interruptions. On Friday evenings, I would often see the five original Lima Lama board members (Tino's first five official students). They received special board members-only training. They practiced in the garage while I waited inside the house. Tino would later explain what he was teaching.

*"Right now, we are working on the rolling block,"* he would say. *"Sometimes we'd practice one technique for hours or days."*

The rolling block was a circular type of block utilized in a forward or backward manner.

*"I like to drill them, after that, we practice the techniques at full force and full contact,"* he added.

I was always curious about what Tino was teaching others, especially the five original members. Then again, I knew what they were learning, because we all hailed from the same school. If I saw something different from the old teaching style, I knew it had come from Tino. Those students concentrated on the rolling block, check block, wrist rotations, forms and occasional techniques. I soon mastered the art of observation. I studied them, watched their demonstrations and saw what they were teaching in their school. I would then compare their teaching to the older curriculum they practiced and record the difference. My observation skills became a trusted training partner, helping me with deduction and analysis. I eventually realized that Lima Lama was not being taught as a system but rather as a collection of techniques, which made it even more difficult for instructors to teach the art's pure form.

While each of the original members had been in their respective martial art for a number of years, they were not proficient in their new martial art—Lima Lama. Tino didn't mind if his students/instructors were still teaching their former martial art; he knew it would take time for them to fully *understand* his Lima Lama, yet alone *teach* it. He also realized that transitioning from traditional karate to Lima Lama would come in increments. After all, Lima Lama was a highly complex creation and as such, it was quite understandable that they shed the components of their base style in favor of Lima Lama in a methodical manner. Subsequently, the more they identified with Tino's style, the more Lima Lama found its way into their teaching.

Each time they met for their group class with Tino, the more they were exposed to the power and effectiveness of Lima Lama. The bottom line is that it does not matter what the board members were teaching their students; their curriculum had been permanently altered. Lima Lama little by little was merging with their martial art. Each school eventually integrated the Lima Lama Techniques, movements, and practices.

Sal Esquivel and Richard Nunez taught Kenpo; Tiny Lefiti was Kung-Fu; John Louis and Solomon Kaihewalu, Okinawa-te Karate. Their Kenpo, their Kung-Fu, their Okinawa-te was no longer pure. Lima Lama had now entered the mix—and in a big way.

*As the Master sits alone in his room, Louis opens the door and sticks his head through the opening.*

*"Master I'm back," he announces. "I'm here to see you again and to hear more of your stories. I told my dad about you and he said it would be fine to come see you again, but not to leave the stadium."*

*"Louis come in and let's talk a bit," the Master said, nodding. "But first let's go and get something to drink. I saw a small refreshment counter next to the side door."*

*"Wow, Master, that would be great, let's go," Louis replied. The Master and his new friend walked down to get a drink and then sat on a bench watching the Black Belt Lima Lama forms competition. While the Master is watching the forms, he hears a couple talking to each other. The Master then zooms in on a Lima Lama patch affixed to the right side of the man's uniform. The sight of the patch sends the Master's mind wandering. This time it involves how Tino and Claire met, how they fell in love and how they married years later.*

# Chapter 9
## Tino and Claire

**Hawaii 1952**

I remember waiting in the living room before my lessons with Tino. Sometimes one of Tino's daughters would keep me company. But most often I was joined by his wife, Claire, who was a fountain of information on everything from the way Tino taught his Lima Lima to the state of their family. It was also common for Claire to share stories about her husband. She admitted that Tino was a charmer and had his own way of handling family situations. He knew what to do or what to say to keep her from becoming too angry or disappointed when things did not go her way.

At the same time, she could identify his faults. Sometimes Claire would talk about his behaviour, his temper, or even other women. Though he had a habit of making her angry, it was evident she felt a great deal of love and admiration for him. When Tino came into a room, she would quickly stand and give him a chair. And then she would bring Tino food or drink. She catered to his every need with a genuine devotion. She remained in contact even after their divorce. It was a love she held until her last breath.

This love story has a unique beginning. It was 1952, just 11 years after the surprise attack on Pearl Harbor by the Japanese and seven years since Japan's ultimate unconditional surrender on the U.S.S.

Battleship Missouri. The impact of the Korean conflict was still being felt throughout the world. To make matters worse, Hawaii experienced a great Tsunami in 1952, which caused immense devastation.

These events clearly had their effect upon the culture of the day. It was during this era that 19-year-old Claire first laid eyes on Tino at a Marine dance in Pearl Harbor, HI. It was only natural that a young man would approach an attractive young girl like Claire and ask her to dance. Much to his surprise she promptly turned him down.

She saw him a second time while attending a Marine boxing match with a girlfriend. Tino was on the card that night and it was his boxing skills that impressed her.

Claire remembered telling her girlfriend that Tino was an important person, because he was the middleweight *all Pacific Champion.* Claire remembered that after the boxing event she saw Tino with another girl outside the arena. That's when she vowed to *make him mine.* At another dance the following week, Tino and Claire saw each other again. But this time she was with a date. Claire gave Tino a warm glance and he returned the greeting. When Tino noticed that her date had stepped outside the dance hall, he walked over to Claire and asked her to dance. She accepted and as they danced Tino asked if they could meet later in the evening. She told him to follow her home after the dance and they could meet at the side of her house after the date left. That was their first official date. That evening Claire told him not to call her home because her mother did not approve of her dating a Samoan military man. Claire's mom did not think a Samoan man in uniform was interested in a serious relationship.

They agreed to meet a few days at a nearby corner and as time went by Tino and Claire became a serious relationship. Despite Claire's warning, one day Tino called the house. When no one answered the phone, Tino thought Claire was out with another man. So he hopped in a military Jeep and drove to her house. He was carrying a fully loaded machine gun as he burst into her house and finding no one at home. It was so embarrassing when Claire's mom found out what happen.

*"I tell you Albert he was a very jealous man, very controlling and possessive,"* Claire remembers.

There were problems even when they were on a date. She recalled an incident at a dance after they started dating. She refused to dance with him because nobody was on the dance floor and he was drunk. He then became angry, told her that if she wouldn't dance with him, nobody would dance. He then went to the platform where the band was playing and violently kicked the drums off the platform. The kick was so hard that he dented the front cover of the base drum frame. The military police were called, but as fate had have it, the bar owner was a Samoan friend of Tino's, so no charges were pressed. Not to mention the military police also knew Tino; since he was popular among his Marine peers because of his boxing reputation. He was both admired for his talents and feared for his temper. Tino was a jealous man, as he would get stirred up if a man even looked at Claire he threatened to beat up the man if he didn't keep his eyes to himself. Claire admitted that at the time she was too young to recognize how controlling Tino was. Ironically, what drove Claire into Tino's arms in the first place was her mother's controlling nature. Claire explained it as, *"Going from the frying pan into the fire. I didn't know better."*

Tino proposed after the pair had dated a few months, but Claire's mom refused to allow the marriage. Tino was insistent and after nine months of asking, Claire finally relented. They married in 1953, had children in 1954, 1955 and 1956, rested in 1957, and then had more children in 1958, 1960, 1961 and 1962.

*The Master remembers Tino's recollection about joining the Marines in 1947 at the age 17.*

As we sat in the front room I asked Tino about his date of birth. He turned to me and said, "*It's kind of funny Al. I got two different birth years. In Samoa there was no original birth certificate for me. My mother gave birth to me at home and they never registered my date of birth. I was actually born in 1930, but my legal birth certificate says 1931.*"

"*I don't understand,*" I said.

Tino continued. "*When I left Samoa to study in Hawaii, I didn't like going to school, so I decided to join the Marines. I was 17 and wasn't eligible to join the Marines because I was not 18 years old. That was the legal age for the Military. So I went back to Samoa and got my parents to get me a false birth certificate. My father went to the recording office and put 1931 as my year of birth. That made me 18. That's how I got to join the Marines.*"

"*Wow you've got two birthdays,*" I said to Tino.

He smiled at me and said, "*Ya, but now I have to use my registered birth year. Funny right?*"

Back at the Stadium

*The Master turns his attention toward the forms competition. He witnesses a Lima Lama Black Belt doing a weapons form. The competitor is twirling a staff with his hands as part of routine. Suddenly, the Master imagines flames exploding from the staff as he recalls stories of Tino performing a fiery routine.*

# Chapter 10
## Fire Dancer

Tino received an honorable discharge from the Marines in 1955. Shortly after his discharge, he attended the University of Hawaii and was earning $160 a month from the government (for attending school) and was paying $150 tuition. The couple was struggling financially so Tino found employment at a big hotel as a Hawaiian knife and fire dancer. The pay was $150 a week.

*"When Tino makes up his mind about something, he does it,"* Claire related.

Claire could clearly see that Tino was serious about being a professional dancer. He practiced his knife movements by twirling a piece of broom. After a couple of months, Tino went to a junk yard and cut a piece of rusted steel metal from a junk car and shaped it into a large knife. Then he visited a local steel shop. There he had it cleaned, chromed and outfitted with a handle. Tino practiced with that beautiful knife day and night until he became a master knife and fire dancer. He then got a job in a Hawaiian hotel as a professional knife and fire dancer.

# Chapter 11
## Moving to California

In 1958, Tino had a wife and four children to support. His time in the Marines was over and his hotel job was cut to part-time. He sent his family to stay with his mother in American Samoa while he headed for greener employment pastures in California. He moved in with a cousin and found a job with a Los Angeles-based manufacturing company. Tino looked for an apartment for his family, but his rough looks and accent made it difficult to secure a place to live.

Claire was summoned to Los Angeles and eventually found a place for her family. Surprisingly, it was the same apartment that management had just told Tino was already rented. Claire, who was waiting in the car, had suspected something was not right after Tino returned to the car and told her the apartment was already rented. She became suspicious and decided to inquire about the same apartment. They told her it was available and when she informed them her husband had just been there, the owners had no choice but to give in. After a short time living in Los Angeles, Tino and Claire then sent for their four children who were living in Samoa. A few years later, Tino and Claire welcomed three more children into the fold. Fortunately, Tino was made supervisor at the manufacturing company.

Eventually Tino moved his family to the city of San Gabriel where Tino met Ed Parker.

Back at the refreshment counter, the Master is drinking water and watching the martial arts event. The stadium is filled with thousands of Lima Lama Practitioners and visitors. He is amazed at the number of Lima Lama patches embedded on their uniforms. While each uniform color might be different, one important thing is the same: Tino's martial art creation—Lima Lama—can be found on the chest of every stylist.

*What Tino created was unbelievable. To think I was with him from the very beginning of his creation," the Master thought to himself. "Amazing, I can still remember the story of how Tino started in Kenpo Karate and Kung-Fu. It was Claire who told me how he met Mr. Parker in the early 1960s and later how he fostered an association with Kung-Fu Grandmaster Ark Wong.*

## Chapter 12
## Tino Meets Ed Parker

While they were living in San Gabriel, Claire worked as an assistant nurse and Tino held a steady job at a manufacturing company. One day, Tino noticed an advertisement for an Asian martial arts school where Kenpo Karate was being taught. This ad caught his attention, especially because the school was located a few minutes away in Pasadena. When Claire saw the advertisement, she immediately told her husband,

*"Tino, I know the instructor, and the owner of this Kenpo Karate School, Ed Parker."*

Claire explained that the man who married them was Mr. Parker's father. Talk about your coincidence. Even more amazing was that Claire's cousin and Ed Parker were close friends. Tino became interested, visited the Kenpo school, met Mr. Parker and enrolled. This meeting between two future giants changed the course of martial arts history. Neither could have imagined they someday would become martial arts legends.

Ed Parker was credited with bringing the Hawaiian Chinese Kenpo Karate style to America. He trained in Kenpo in Hawaii in the late 1940's under William K.S. Chow, a Chinese martial artist. Ed Parker opened his first Dojo (school) in Pasadena, CA, in 1956 and eventually became known as the "Father of American Karate."

Tino and Parker quickly bonded because they shared Hawaiian roots. Parker soon realized that Tino was far from the typical walk-in student. In fact, right from the start Tino showed his teacher that he had the skills to become a great master. Tino possessed uncanny fighting prowess and quickly rose through the ranks in Parker's revolutionary system. It typically took two years for a new student to achieve brown belt status in Kenpo Karate. Tino accomplished this feat in less than a year! Training hard and fighting were ingrained in Tino's character. His passion for learning propelled him to the head of the class. He would practice every day before and after work. He would even work out during his breaks. His experience as a Marine Corps boxer gave him a noticeable advantage over other students during the Kenpo sparring sessions. Recognizing the potential, Mr. Parker pushed Tino even harder in class. Claire told me that Tino was the one student who sparred all the time, meaning he would face everyone in class, one after another, without breaks.

**The Kenpo Karate Journey**

Naturally, Tino took a beating but he never complained, a trait Parker admired in his students. Tino enjoyed the challenge of becoming better than the next guy. When he finally became a brown belt, Parker gave Tino the responsibility of teaching the Black Belt classes! Tino eventually became Ed Parker's right-hand man.

Parker also leaned on Tino to handle disputes that needed to be settled with a *"strong arm."* When a Black Belt from a competing school requested a challenge, it was Tino who answered the call even though he was wearing a brown belt. Tino would play it cool as the sparring session began. But if the visitor became aggressive Tino would put the martial artist in his place with a beating he would not forget. In one instance Tino really lost his temper with the challenger and Parker had to order four of his students to tackle Tino, take him to the ground and lay on top of him in order to control him. There's another story about a former Parker Black Belt who was bad-mouthing his former instructor. Tino saw him at a local karate tournament and followed him into the men's room. Tino hit him in the face so hard that he flew against the wall and slumped, nearly unconscious, to the floor. Tino then dragged him across the floor, shoved his head into a water bucket and told him, "If you ever say anything bad about Mr. Ed Parker or the Kenpo organization I will have another session with you." Naturally the bad-mouthing stopped.

During his early years in the martial arts it was typical of Tino to first let his fists and temper do the talking. Only later were matters settled with words of understanding. Tino firmly believed that only through the power of fear would respect be achieved. Unfortunately, that same philosophy came back to haunt him years later when it caused problems with family and friends.

**GM Tino Tuiolosega and GM Ed Parker**

# Chapter 13
## Studying Under Kung-Fu Grandmaster Ark Wong

Tino benefited greatly from his two years of study with Master Ed Parker. It was also during his second year of training with Mr. Parker that an event would change Tino's martial arts journey. The timing could not have been better for Tino. Tiny Lefiti, a student and cousin of Tino's, arranged an introduction with Grandmaster (GM) Ark Wong. GM Ark Wong, credited with being the first Chinese to teach non-chinese in America, made a lasting impression on Tino.

GM Wong came to the United States in 1921 and opened schools in San Francisco and Oakland. Later, he came to Los Angeles where he opened his third Kung-Fu school in the city's Chinatown. GM Wong was born in Canton, China, in the village of Toysun Tien Sum Chien, to a family of moderate means. As a boy he lived on his grandfather's farm. At age seven he began studying Choy Lay Fut Kung-Fu under Master Lam Ark Fun at the original Shaolin Temple. His training also included the Chinese healing arts, which he mastered early in his teens.

Ark Wong taught the style of the five families—Choy, Li, Fut, Mok and Hung. He also taught Sil Lum (Cantonese term for the Shaolin Five Animals)—Dragon, Tiger, Snake, Leopard and Crane. This master's wealth of knowledge included teaching Tai Chi Quan, Five-Element Fist, and Hop Gar Lama, along with 18 traditional Shaolin weapons. His wealth of knowledge was to be both appreciated and admired.

Tiny knew early on that GM Wong would be a wonderful teacher for Tino and a superb addition to his cousin's martial arts education. Recognized as a potential teacher for his talented cousin, Tino soon submerged himself into the Chinese martial arts. Now Tino had two teachers. He continued his second year with Master Parker and added a mountain of training in the Chinese martial arts with GM Wong. Tino had an unquenchable thirst for learning. Tiny Lefiti was instrumental in shaping Tino's martial arts destiny. He not only introduced Tino to GM Ark Wong, he paid for private lessons with the Kung-Fu great.

One might question why Tiny paid for Tino's training? During the course of Tiny's Kung-Fu training, he encountered difficulty with some of the moves required to perform the sequences. Tiny's size and weight prohibited him from making the difficult jumps and leaps inherent in advanced Kung-Fu. Undaunted, Tiny used perseverance, dedication, discipline, talent and ingenuity, to gain Kung-Fu Master status. On the other hand, Tino had the perfect body for Kung-Fu's aerial demands. He was already in great physical condition and was still young enough to quickly memorize and perform every move he was taught. When it came to learning Tino was a sponge. GM Wong was so impressed by Tino's fighting ability and learning skills that he brought in four Kung-fu Grandmasters from different styles to continue teaching Tino. At the end of his training, this Samoan demonstrated the courage, persistence, discipline, intelligence, and talent to earn the title Grandmaster. GM Wong and the other Grandmasters signed and conferred Tino's Grandmaster Degree (diploma) in the Five Animal and Five Family styles. This was the first time such a distinguished title had ever been granted to a non-Chinese man!

I once asked Tino, "*why he had been accepted as a non-Chinese man (being a Samoan) and taught Kung-Fu at such a high Master level?*"

"*I told GM Wong I was one-quarter Chinese from my mother's side and that was good enough him,*" Tino related, smiling.

Tino took advantage of the opening to increase his ability and learn from some of the world's foremost teachers.

Grand Master Tino with GM Ark Wong, second Floor to Ark Wong's Kung-fu School in China Town Los Angeles California

302 Ord St - Rear Entrance to GM Wong's School

Danny Inosontos, Tino, Ark Wong, Darnell Garcia, John Yee, Doug Wong Eric Lee and Daniel Lee

# Chapter 14
## The Tiger Form

### Back in Time—From the Arena to Tino's House

*From his seat in the stadium the master looks at a competitor performing the Tiger form. The Master starts to move his hands, as if performing his version of Tiger form. His mind thinks back to when he saw Tino perform the advanced master version of the Tiger.*

I find myself transported to my teacher's home, where I am getting a lesson.

*"What are the distinctions between my Kung-Fu forms and yours?"* I ask.

Tino looks at me and smiles. *"Watch, I'll do the Tiger form so you can see the differences."*

He moves to the center of the room and starts his advanced Tiger form.

*"Ah,"* I said to myself, *"I see the difference now."*

I now know how I can change my Tiger form to make it look like his. He stops a minute into his routine. It is as clear as a bell. I later realized that Tino taught by using himself as an example.

After seeing his precise, sharp, quick and powerful movements, I recalled that Tino had promised his Chinese masters that he would participate and collaborate in master Ark Wong's Kung-Fu organization. Considering Tino's amazing talent it was reasonable that those in GM Wong's group expect him to share his skills. In fact, GM Ark Wong wanted Tino to inherit his martial arts legacy. Tino, however, had other plans, which included creating the art of Lima Lama or the Polynesian art of self-defense.

As the Master sits silently in the Stadium, Louis touches him on the shoulder and asks, *"Can you tell me how you met Grandmaster Tino?"*

*"Is that what you want to know?"* I asked.

*"Oh yes Master, please tell me."* He replied.

*"I'll tell you how I first met him."* I said.

# Chapter 15
## Meeting Mr. Tino Tuiolosega

Meeting Tino Tuiolosega was absolutely the most pivotal time in my life. I had been training for some time at Danny Guzman's Kenpo Karate in Monterey Park. In those days moving through belt rankings was not very easy. Requirements and testing were often quite demanding. I was blessed to learn Kenpo Karate and by the age of 16, I had already worked up to green belt. When it came to teaching martial arts traditions things were different. Students in that era would show a sign of respect and appreciation for their teacher, their school, and fellow students. After all, one learns the art of self-defense to protect what is most precious to us: our lives and the lives of our loved ones. We would bow upon entering the school training area, bow to our teacher, and bow to our fellow classmates in the martial arts school. While we were encouraged to have fun at the school, it was also a place where the serious pursuit of self-defense was first and foremost. However, things were quite different one night as I arrived for karate class. To my surprise, I noticed two young children playing on the sparring mats. They appeared to be about five and seven years of age. Since I had interacted with numerous ethnicities throughout my life, these playful children appeared to be Samoan or of Samoan ethnicity. Mr. Guzman prohibited children to be inside the training area. So I was pretty shocked at the sight of these kids enjoying themselves. (I later learned the names of these kids were Myron and Kaipo.)

Further down the training area was Mr. Guzman's office. I could see Mr. Guzman was with a gentleman I did not recognize. He appeared to be in his early 30s and wore a starched white Karate gi with a patch that read "Ed Parker Kenpo." Around his waist was a Brown Belt (one rank below the Black Belt level). What was most noticeable about him was his stature. He was at least 6 feet tall and powerfully built. I later discovered the man they simply called "Tino" had visited our school to promote Ed Parker's Kenpo style and organization and to train with our advanced class—students holding brown and Black Belt ranks.

I changed into my karate uniform and by the time I returned to the training area Tino was already sparring with one of the school's Black Belts. It was strange to see a brown belt easily controlling a higher-ranking Black Belt. Even more interesting was that Tino was sparring with a man who had recently finished second in the middleweight sparring division at the Long Beach International Tournament (Ed Parker's event). That evening Tino sparred "nonstop" with each of the Black Belts at the school. Clearly, Tino was just playing and not putting any real effort into his attacks. It was evident he could easily have hurt his opponents. Tino had a strong presence about him; he assumed a short boxing stance with his hands up. His stance was radically different from the karate stance to which I was accustomed. Our posture featured a long wide stance with a hand guard of one hand up and the other hand protecting the midsection. Our attacks were tensed and we struck only to the body. Also uncommon was his use of the front leg for a straight kick. Most karate stylists fired with the rear leg. I noticed that he was relaxed then tensed when he executed his attacking movements. When he showed aggressiveness, I not only saw the power, but I also could sense the speed and destruction in his strikes. After thanking each student for their time, he remained following class to demonstrate more of Ed Parker's self-defense techniques. I was stunned by his performance: In all my years of training in boxing, judo and karate, I had never seen anything like it. Tino was impressive, to say the least!

## Tino—The Kenpo Karate Brown Belt

Remarkably, Tino's impact is still felt today. The power and speed he showed at Dan Guzman's School resonates inside me every time I step on the training room floor. We spoke after class that fateful day and in passing I happened to notice he had a rather large thumbnail—far beyond normal size (the rest of his nails were normal size). When I question him about his thumbnail, Tino responded by extending his right hand toward my face and inching his nail in front of my eye.

*"That's for poking the eye,"* he admitted.

It was much later that I learned from my teacher, Mr. Guzman, that Tino was Mr. Parker's right-hand man, charged with promoting Mr. Parker's Kenpo style by visiting different schools and sparring with all the Black Belts. It's possible that Tino's brown belt put teachers of other karate schools at ease and more receptive.

## The Master in the Stadium

*As the Master and Louis watch the Lima Lama event, Louis interjects, "Look Master, that's my brother doing the form and that's my dad and mom watching. The Master motions for Louis to join them.*

*"Louis you should be there supporting your brother like your dad and mom. Go, then come back later and I'll tell you more stories."*

*Louis rushes to his brother's corner. The Master rises from his seat, returns to his waiting room and begins to stretch.*

I always thank God for my good health and the gifts I have discovered through martial arts. However, even as I prepare for my demonstration, I cannot ignore the profound impact Tino has had on me. During my youth I saw Tino as being indestructible until one day I saw him incapacitated.

# Chapter 16
## Tino's First Heart Attack

The year was 1971 and Tino was brimming with energy and determination. He was serious about achieving his goals, proving whether it meant furthering the education of his inner circle or attracting skeptics who doubted the effectiveness of his style. In a word, Tino's demonstrations were dynamic. In fact, in some cases they were *too* powerful as his students could attest. Tino's tough-as-nails approach took its toll on giver and receiver alike. During one of his demonstrations in Diamond Bar, CA. the seemingly indestructible one proved he was human after all when he suffered a mild heart attack.

Sometimes life teaches us painful lessons and this was a tough one for Tino to handle. I remember calling his home to make an appointment for my usual private lesson when his daughter, Kim, answered and gave me the bad news: Tino was in the hospital. The news left me numb and speechless. All I could think about was Tino and how his family was dealing with the news.

*"This can't be,"* I told myself. Tino was as strong as an ox, a mountain of a man who wore invincibility like a badge of courage. I learned a valuable lesson that day—if a person as strong as Tino could be hurt, then anyone was vulnerable. The man I so admired for his power and speed was flat on his back in a hospital bed. For the

first time Tino was more than a teacher; he was a trusted friend and member of my family.  As much as I wanted to see him, I waited a few days to visit Tino in the hospital. I called his house the following day and asked Claire if Tino was accepting visitors. She thanked me for my concern but suggested I give Tino a few days to rest. One week later I headed for the hospital.

**Tino at the Hospital**

He was listed in stable condition when I finally got to see him but he was not out of the woods. I walked into his room, nodded in a friendly manner. He looked weak and fragile, but I tried to keep the mood positive.

"*How are you feeling?*" I asked.

"*I'm not feeling too well but I'll be OK. I had a mild heart attack and they're giving me some medicine to make my heart get better.*" Tino laughed softly and said, "*I'm still working out even here in the hospital. The nurse caught me practicing the rolling check blocks in the bathroom and she got pretty angry with me for not resting.*"

Typical Tino, I thought. I nodded like I understood, but deep down I appreciated the nurse's concern. She was serious about his recovery, even though Tino's focus remained on his Lima Lama. I reminded Tino that he had to tone down his practice time so no one would discover what he was doing. Tino and I talked briefly about our families and then he stared at me with a serious look in his eyes.

*"Do you remember, you asked me about the finger sets, the pressure points?"* Tino asked.

*"Yes,"* I replied. *"You told me that someday when it was the right time you'd show me the pressure point applications."*

*"This is the right time,"* Tino responded. *"You never know what will happen next. Look at where I'm at."*

I understood what he was saying and why he thought now was the perfect time. Tino rose from his prone position and started showing me his first set of finger pressure points. At first I felt uneasy because the last thing I wanted during my visit was to make him work. To my surprise, Tino the martial arts instructor was back and demonstrating the Lima Lama finger pressure point sets. I went along with Tino's intentions and listened attentively to his instruction.

*"Al, keep this to yourself; it is too dangerous for others to know,"* he said, cautioning me. *"This is the death touch that has existed in the Chinese martial arts for thousands of years. It's even more deadly because I adapted it to Lima Lama by modifying it and making it more effective."*

I promised I would guard his secret. I felt privileged that he trusted me with such important information. I understood the responsibility I carried to guard what I learned with my life.

My hospital visits to see Tino were nothing less than life changing because they dealt with so much more than martial arts. The visits spoke to me about what really mattered: God, life, family, friends and health.

# Chapter 17
## The Call From Elvis Presley

It was Tino's third week at the hospital and I was the last visitor of the day. I could tell Tino was glad to see me.

*"Guess who called me last night?"* he said excitedly.

*"I don't know."* I responded.

*"Elvis Presley"* Tino answered.

*"Really? You know Elvis?"* I asked.

*"No, no I don't know him personally,"* he replied. *"Did you know that Ed Parker is Elvis' martial arts teacher and bodyguard? Ed called me last night and let me know that he was talking with Elvis about me and about my condition here at the hospital. So Elvis told Ed that he would try and stop by to see me this week. But Elvis called me last night and said he couldn't stop by to see me because he had some business to take care of. But that he just wanted to say hello and to wish me well."*

*"Wow,"* I said. *"That's really nice of Mr. Presley to call you."*

Tino then smiled and said,

*"Yeah! And I told all the nurses, before the call that Elvis might stop by to say hello. They all just started to giggle. The nurses also said they would tell their friends about it."*

I could see that Tino was thrilled about Elvis calling him that evening and I was certain this was all true considering the close friendship he had with Ed Parker.

Tino softly laughed and said, *"I better tell them that he is not coming and that he just called me to wish me well."*

*Back at the Stadium, the Master was thinking about Tino's brush with fame.*

Elvis Presley was a serious martial artist and highly respected Ed Parker. In fact, most people do not realize that Elvis often practiced Karate with his bodyguards and that he was a legitimate Karate practitioner. Some of his Las Vegas shows actually featured Kenpo Karate demonstrations.

Practicing Karate at his home or at the dojo with those close to him, including Ed Parker provided Elvis a break from the pressures of performing. Elvis could leave entertainment behind and focus on another discipline: Karate. I remember seeing a video documentary of Elvis preparing and rehearsing for his concerts in Las Vegas. I was in awe of his discipline, his deep concentration, focus and dedication, knowledge of music, all-around competency, and attention to detail. It would only seem natural that Elvis would place the same emphasis on his Karate training. He applied himself to Ed Parker's Kenpo system and became a legitimate high-ranking Black Belt practitioner.

Elvis could have chosen any martial arts teacher in the world. Why did he choose Ed Parker? Elvis recognized Ed Parker's talent. Elvis Presley and Ed Parker developed a sincere friendship based on their common interest in the martial arts and entertainment business. When Ed Parker shared concern for Tino Tuiolosega's condition, as a response, Elvis Presley showed compassion for Tino Tuiolosega. Elvis then called Tino in the hospital to express his concern for the Grandmaster.

Tino met a number of celebrities, artists and screen actors thanks to his association with Ed Parker, who taught many Hollywood celebrities. One celebrity was a talented young martial artist from San Francisco, who was taking the entertainment industry by storm through a combination of charisma and exceptional kung-fu skill. This man was none other than Bruce Lee.

# Chapter 18
## The Bruce Lee Friendship

I received my first formal training in Kenpo Karate from Dan Guzman. Guzman would later relocate his dojo from East Los Angeles to the neighboring city of Monterey Park. After his move, Mr. Guzman began taking private lessons from Ed Parker, who at the time was one of the hottest teachers on the West Coast. He was a martial arts genius who could relate his style to the masses. Dan Guzman was no exception. He learned Kenpo from Parker and dedicated himself to enhancing his skills with the Hawaiian genius.

One of the traits that set Parker apart was his willingness to share his knowledge. It was common to find his house in Pasadena filled every night with martial artists of all styles and ranks. One of those martial artists was Bruce Lee, a friend and frequent houseguest. Known first for his role in the TV series "The Green Hornet" and later through his Shaw Brothers movies, Lee loved to surround himself with fans of the arts. It was at Parker's house one night that Dan Guzman traded handshakes with the "Little Dragon" himself.

Later I would enjoy a similar pleasure when I met Bruce Lee and discovered the camaraderie he shared with my teacher, Tino Tuiolosega.

**The Mysterious Motorcycle Rider**

One Wednesday night while I was training at Dan Guzman's Karate School in Monterey Park, I heard the sound of a motorcycle in the parking lot. I momentarily interrupted my Karate workout to see what was making all that noise. I saw a young man in a helmet wearing a black leather jacket. The gentlemen riding the motorcycle parked in front of our school. Curiosity got the better of me and I took a break to see the visitor. As he removed his helmet, I remember raising my voice and announcing,

*"Hey, that's Bruce Lee outside and he's coming in!" I stared at Mr. Guzman and he acknowledged that coming into the dojo was, indeed, Bruce Lee. "Yes that's him,"* he said.

I approached Bruce Lee, introduced myself and invited him to say a word to my classmates. We exchanged greetings and then he agreed to sign autographs. He was cordial, spoke with us for a while and then went inside Mr. Guzman's office. I was surprised at Bruce's stature. He was about 5-feet-7 inches and rather slim. He was polite, quiet, almost shy, but very accommodating when it came to answering questions or signing his name to anything we had. Bruce remained at the school for a while and then left on his motorcycle. We found out later that Bruce Lee was staying at Mr. Parker's home, while frequently visiting Ed's school in Pasadena. It was the same school at which Tino trained. As fate would have it, Tino and Bruce became good friends. Bruce was said to be impressed with Tino's abilities and leadership qualities after watching him teach.

# Los Angeles California China Town

# Bruce Lee's School In Los Angeles China Town
## Al Garza in front of Bruce Lee's school door

# Chapter 19

## Tino's Hawaiian Luau Birthday

Tino loved birthdays and chose to celebrate his 1968 version with a Hawaiian luau-themed party inside the San Gabriel Auditorium. Part of the entertainment was a Jeet Kune Do demonstration by Bruce Lee. Later that evening, Tino performed his Lima Lama demonstration. His students Richard Nunez and Sal Esquivel assisted him. Bruce and Tino's martial arts exhibitions were greatly anticipated by everyone and when I close my eyes I can still feel the excitement in the air.

When Tino was planning his Luau celebration, he made it a point to invite his friend and martial arts brother, Bruce Lee. Bruce was more than happy to oblige and offered to perform a demonstration. This says a lot about the respect Bruce had for Tino. Even though Bruce was becoming a worldwide celebrity, he still had time for those who shared his martial arts passion. The respect was mutual; the night before the Luau party Tino and Claire visited Bruce at his school in Los Angeles' Chinatown. They arrived to find Dan Inosanto running the class. While they waited they noticed Dan striking the traditional Chinese drums using sound and tempo to guide the students' movements.

When Bruce arrived they all discussed the following evening's Luau event. At the Luau party, Bruce sat with Ed Parker and Tino. And before Tino's demonstration, Bruce walked onstage and performed his famous two-finger push-ups. Bruce's physical prowess was extraordinary. He followed up by firing a few fast kicks at an assistant and then finished with a mind-blowing two-inch punch to the chest. The blow sent his assistant flying backward.

Bruce climbed off the stage and met the crowd, signing autographs for an appreciative throng. This was a monumental event for those in attendance and showed people how much Bruce Lee thought of Tino.

It was no surprise that Bruce eventually made a name for himself as a great actor, great martial artist and innovator. Tino admired and valued Bruce's talent. Tino got what he wanted for his birthday: Bruce Lee as his special guest! Both Tino and Bruce delivered awesome and extraordinary martial arts exhibitions—Bruce's Jeet Kune Do or "*Way of the Intercepting Fist*", and Tino's Lima Lama or "*Hand of Wisdom.*"

About 30 minutes after Bruce's electrifying performance we were all in high spirits. However, there remained a great feeling of anticipation for Tino's upcoming demonstration. Sal Esquivel was Tino's first assistant. Sal assumed a fighting stance with his hands forward and without warning fired a full-force shot toward Tino's face. Reacting with speed and amazing force, Tino leveled a counterstrike that actually contacted Sal's face. It was pretty ugly. The audience was shocked by what happened next. At the precise moment of contact, a small object flew from Sal's mouth. It was his tooth. Tino hit his assistant so hard that he managed to dislodge one of his permanent side teeth. At that moment the audience was silent as Tino continued. I thought to myself,

*"This guy (Sal) is tough, he's got courage,"*

Yet, Sal acted as if nothing was wrong, continuing with the next technique.

Next up was Richard Nunez. This time I noticed a bit of hesitation in Richard's walk. He was to throw a punch at Tino. Instead, he slowly walked up to Tino and asked him to take it easy. Richard punched and instinctively bounced backward before Tino could reach him. The crowd roared laughing, thinking it was all an act. No one knew Richard was in "survivor" mode. It was hard to blame Richard or Sal for being a bit apprehensive. They knew from experience that someone might be getting hurt.

Today, when I drive past the corner of Valley & San Gabriel Boulevards where that Auditorium stood, I still think of Tino, Bruce, Sal, Richard and the Hawaiian Luau Birthday Celebration. What an amazing moment in martial arts history.

# At San Gabriel Luau Birthday Celebration

**Courtesy Picture by Richard Nunez**

**Mrs. Nunez   Bruce Lee   Richard Nunez**

*Louis approaches the Master and taps him on the shoulder.*

*"Master, are you OK?" Louis asks. "You haven't said a word for awhile."*

*"Oh, I'm sorry Louis. I was just daydreaming about my past with Grandmaster Tino and Lima Lama."*

*Louis prods the Master for more information. "Please tell me Master, I want to know what you were thinking."*

*"Well, what would you like to know?"*

*"Tell me when Lima Lama started?"*

*The stadium becomes empty as Louis hears the Master's voice explain the official beginning of Lima Lama.*

Lima Lama began in 1965 following the break-up between Tino and Ed Parker. According to Claire, Tino and Parker had agreed to become partners in Ed's Kenpo Karate Organization. Something, however, made Ed change his mind about the partnership. Tino decided to form an organization and teach his new self-defense system (and style) called Lima Lama, the "Hands of Wisdom." It was Tino who named it Lima Lama and it was Tino who formed the Lima Lama Organization. Later that year, Tino gathered his first board members: Tiny, Richard, Sal, John, and finally, Solomon.

# Chapter 20
## The First Six Board Members

Tino's five original Lima Lama board members were also his students: Tiny Lefiti, Richard Nunez, Sal Esquivel, John Louis, and Solomon Kaihewalu.

**Courtesy Picture by Richard Nunez**

MEMBERS OF THE FIRST LIMALAMA ASSOCIATION

**Richard Nunez  John Louis  Sal Esquivel  Solomon Kaihewalu**
**Grandmaster Tino Tuiolosega and Tiny Lefiti**

## Sal and Richard

I met Sal Esquivel and Richard Nunez in March 1965 when I began studying Karate with Mr. Dan Guzman. His first Karate Dojo was at a community building called the "Cleveland House," also known as the East Los Angeles basketball gym. Mr. Guzman's held Karate classes Mondays and Wednesdays.

### Cleveland House Early 1965

**Left side - Sal Esquivel third from the top row, Dan Guzman left side third from the bottom row. Ed Parker fourth from Bottom Row**

## Sal Esquivel

Mr. Esquivel was a Mexican-American who resided in El Monte, CA., a city east of Los Angeles. He was an electrician by day and a martial artist teacher by night. He also was a competitive body builder and despite a 5-foot-7, 190-pound frame, he was in peak physical condition. He was an athlete in the true sense of the word.

Karate was Sal's passion. He taught it part-time in the evening through the parks and recreation department and received little, if any remuneration. He did it because he loved it. On Tuesdays and Thursdays, Sal was at State School gym near Hazard Park, where at times I would also train. Sal was still a brown belt, but already teaching and sharing his knowledge of Karate. This man was truly dedicated to learning and teaching Karate. When Mr. Guzman relocated his school to the city of Monterey Park, Sal (and Richard Nunez) followed him. They both would later meet Tino at various Karate tournaments. However, the manner in which Sal met Tino had an interesting and unique twist.

An Interesting point was that Tino while still with Ed Parker's organization visited both gentlemen at their own commercial Karate schools and enlisted them as members of his Lima Lama organization and at Tinos request each of the original members of Tino Tuiolosega's Lima Lama Organization signed a formal acknowledgment pledging their allegiance as Tino's students.

**Sal the Competitor**

Sal was a straightforward fighter on the tournament circuit and a powerhouse who did not back down to anyone. Sal was an unbeatable combination of strength, talent, and courage. A case in point: Sal met Tino at a Karate tournament *the hard way*. He was almost knocked out by the future Grandmaster. Ironically, Tino was disqualified for hitting Sal in the head. Tino was too fast for Sal and Sal never knew what hit him. As Sal went to punch, Tino countered with a shot to the head that staggered his opponent. Sal went to his knees. Judges disqualified Tino for excessive force. Tino's blows must have scared and shocked the tournament referees, as well as the audience witnessing the fight.

Granted, the punch cost Tino an automatic disqualification. However, much more came out of this traumatic and painful experience. In the midst of the terrible pain and confusion, Sal realized that Tino had skills that he wanted to learn. Sal never met anyone during his tournament days who could handle his aggressive power style of fighting. Sal knew he needed to learn the secrets behind this amazing fighting style. He decided to become Tino's student. Eventually Sal also joined Tino's Lima Lama Organization.

*The Master is explaining to Louis about Sal Esquivel's Techniques.*

Louis, not only was I fortunate to become one of Tino's first students, I was lucky to witness all his senior students in action— either during training or assisting Tino during Lima Lama demonstrations. Sal possessed a wide fighting stance, which he used to fire bursts of rolling punches as he attacked. Sal's repertoire also included a reverse two-knuckle punch to the face that came so quickly his opponent's were powerless to stop it.

Sal also favored kick attacks, preferring to use sidekick or a spinning back kick to score. While friend and classmate, Richard, seldom used kicks, Sal employed kicking maybe 40 percent of the time.

When Sal kicked, he put his all into it! This man would stop for no one. In fact, he never even held back when facing Tino in a Lima Lama demonstration. If Tino commanded him to go hard, Sal would do just that, even though he knew what the outcome might be. Sal almost became accustomed to the pain factor. Richard warned Sal to be more careful when fighting, especially when paired with Tino during a demonstration. Sal only knew one way. Sal was all in when it came to his commitment to Lima Lama.

As time passed, Sal's knowledge as a teacher also expanded. He became more of a technician, exploring Lima Lama as a practitioner and Master. He discovered the finer points of Lima Lama movement and explained the theory behind the sequences to his dedicated students. He approached his new teaching regimen with the same seriousness, care and dedication he had shown in his Karate teaching.

Master Sal left behind a unique legacy of courage and strength of character. He invested time and effort into helping his student's progress in their Lima Lama training. Sal is an example that will always inspire us.

I last saw Sal in the mid-1990's in Pico Rivera, CA. He was teaching Lima Lama at a parks and recreations gym. I went there to videotape him for my World of Martial Arts program. It was nice to see Sal again and as I walked into the gym I noticed he had lost weight. He looked frail and was walking with a cane. He explained that he suffered a job-related accident. Sal worked as an electrician and had touched a live wire. He was now on disability and teaching Lima Lama full-time.

Sal did a Lima Lama demonstration and his advanced students followed suit. After class I interviewed Sal about his early Lima Lama training, how he met Tino and their later relationship. He smiled and then related the story of "beating" Tino in a tournament match. We all knew it was Sal who took the real beating. I thanked Sal and we promised to get together again soon. Sadly, in 1995 Sal died of a heart attack. He was in his late 60s.

*The Master finds the Stadium the perfect place to go back in time.*

I had no idea the "*Cleveland House*" gym would someday become a meeting place where lives would be changed and lifelong friendships would be made. All thanks to Karate lessons. It all started in that little corner of East Los Angeles. I discovered that Richard Nunez was not only a classmate of Sal's, but also a friend who shared a common interest in Karate. Both gentlemen ultimately found a bond in Lima Lama as students of Grandmaster Tino Tuiolosega.

**Richard Nunez**

Richard Nunez was born in 1930 and was from a Mexican-American household in East Los Angeles. He was small in stature, which made him stand out from the other four original board members who were large and powerfully built. Richard stood about 5-foot-7 and checked in at around 140 pounds. He began boxing at the Main Street Gym, but his formal martial arts training started when his brother Frank introduced him to Mr. Dan Guzman at the Cleveland gym in East Los Angeles. Richard soon was hooked on Karate and trained very hard. The Kenpo style he learned in those years was a hard Japanese Karate approach found commonly in Kajukenbo. Ultimately, Richard earned his first Black Belt in Kenpo Karate with Mr. Guzman. Richard was already a Black Belt under Mr. Guzman when I met him at the Cleveland House. Richard was the first of Mr. Guzman's students to open a commercial Karate school in Montebello, CA.

When demonstrating Karate, Richard had fast, quick hands and agile footwork. When he saw Tino performing, however, he realized there was more to martial arts than what he was practicing.

*"I want those hands."* He told Tino. *"I want to have your speed and techniques."*

Tino liked what Richard told him and accepted him as a student, because he saw Richard's personality, ambition and potential. The years went by and Richard progressed in his Lima Lama knowledge and training.

When it came to sparring, everything with Richard was about moving continuously. That was his personality. This meant that Richard was always moving around during a fight. Even when he was not attacking or defending, some part of his body would be moving. Some thought Richard moved that way because he was nervous, but this was not true. Rather than classifying Richard's continuous motion as "nervous energy," it is more accurate to say that Richard used a God-given overflow of energy to his advantage.

Many fighters have successfully used continuous motion as a mode of attack. Prizefighters moved around so they could measure their opponents. I was a keen observer of Richard's movements. The more he moved, the better chance he had of exploiting his opponent's openings. When Richard found his chance, he would attack with three or four consecutive punches. For the most part, Richard did well; when he ran into difficulties he would retreat as quickly as possible. His footwork was remarkable and made his defense even more impressive. He needed the skill because he was commonly facing bigger and stronger opponents.

One side of Richard I will always appreciate is his way with people. He has always been sociable and great conversationalist. When it comes to Lima Lama he is non-stop—all enthusiasm. Richard's face lights up when he explains a technique to his students. However, his upbeat personality reaches a fever pitch when discussing Lima Lama. Spend some time with this gentleman and he will have you listening or laughing to his martial arts experiences.

Grandmaster Richard Nunez continues to teach even into his late 70s and shares his Lima Lama wisdom through a personal touch. You can still catch him flowing through his Lima Lama movements at his Whittier (CA) school. His students continue to carry the torch of Lima Lama throughout California, as well as Mexico.

### John Louis and Solomon Kaihewalu

John Louis was born in South Kona, Hawaii and raised in Damon Track, Honolulu, Hawaii. He was a quiet man who kept to himself. However, he projected a unique confidence and strength, whether it was during Lima Lama practices or when assisting Tino at demonstrations. As a sidelight, when he wasn't teaching martial arts he would take his wife on weekend outings. They would put on their leather jackets and goes motorcycle riding on his Harley-Davidson. John and his wife were free spirits who experienced the beauty of nature by the traveling on motorcycle and creating friendships among their weekend riders' group.

Granted, weekend Harley-Davidson journeys were nothing close to fighting, but this activity gave John an outlet that served him well. The contrast here is that his fighting and martial arts had an entirely different dynamic. The forces at work in his Lima Lama were distinct. Through time I discovered that John had a strong character. He was known for having endured rough training sessions under Tino. I know firsthand that Tino's training and teaching practice sessions were not only rough, but downright dangerous.

John, however, was persistent and that needs to be acknowledged. His steadfast desire to learn could be traced back to a Japanese

Karate background, which emphasizes strength, discipline, and concentration. Before he became a Lima Lama practitioner, John was already deeply involved with an Okinawa Karate style under the instruction of Master Mr. Gordon Doversola.

John dove into his Okinawan training and quickly progressed through the ranks, eventually earning a high-ranking Black Belt. John later opened his own Karate dojo and earned a reputation as a well-respected Master and teacher. For John, however, his martial arts journey took an unexpected turn when he discovered Lima Lama. When John saw Tino demonstrate Lima Lama, he realized that there was something lacking in his training. Like all Masters of others styles, the sight of Tino's speed and power was too much to ignore.

John saw something special in Tino and he wanted it for himself. Louis joined the ranks of Lima Lama converts and eventually became one of Tino's trusted members. John's command of Lima Lama movements was a thing of beauty. His quickness and fierce determination were just what Tino wanted in his fighters. He executed his Lima Lama movements in a classic relaxed manner. John's sacrifice paid off, because he reached the level of expressing Lima Lama the way Tino hoped. Soft, flowing movements transformed into amazing speed and power at the point of impact. John assisted Tino many times during demonstrations and he never held back, even though he knew what was coming. John and Sal were much the same when it came to strength of character. Both were willing to endure personal sacrifice to help their Grandmaster look good. John was a contradiction in terms: in one sense he was a quiet man who enjoyed the serenity of motorcycle riding with his wife; in another sense he was the courageous Lima Lama practitioner who gave everything to Tino and the martial arts style he loved. Tino's Lima Lama Organization grew to four and then to five when John recognized talent in one of his own students—a Hawaiian named Solomon Kaihewalu

John Louis passed away on January 1, 1989 from a heart attack. He was in his late fifties. A Samoan warrior at heart, he embodied the best of what Lima Lama had to offer.

**Solomon Kaihewalu The Fifth Member**
Solomon Kaihewalu was born on Dec. 2, 1935 in what was called the Palama Settlement of Oahu, HI. Solomon started his Karate training under John Louis in the Okinawa-Te system and was then introduced to Lima Lama. Ultimately he became the fifth and final member of Tino's organization. Tino was protective of his system and choosing Solomon meant that he saw something special in the Hawaiian. Even more impressive is that when he joined Lima Lama he had yet to earn his Karate Black Belt. A year after joining the Lima Lama group, Tino promoted Solomon to Black Belt. Tino intensified Solomon's instruction, because he recognized that Solomon was a serious and skilled martial artist.

Solomon spoke about martial arts with a serious reverence. He was very well respected, not only by his fellow students but also by the other Lima Lama practitioners. And so it was a bit surprising that Solomon became the first to leave the Tino's organization and follow a different martial arts path. His ambition paid off a few years later when he founded Ohana Lua, Kaihewalu style. Today, he continues to share his wisdom with a large group of dedicated students.

**Haumea F. "Tiny" Lefiti: The first Original Lima Lama Member**
Haumea "Tiny" Lefiti introduced Tino to Kung-Fu Grandmaster Ark Wong and later paid to have him receive private lessons. Haumea "Tiny" Lefiti was a true, close friend of Tino's—so close in fact, they called each other cousins. Tino brought Tiny along during his second visit to Dan Guzman's school. Tiny was not the least bit "tiny," as his 6-foot-4, 250-pound Samoan frame would attest. Tiny had a special quality about him. He was a big man with an even bigger heart. Inside that mammoth chest beat the heart of a caring, compassionate man.

I met Tiny Lefiti in 1965 while he was sitting inside Mr. Guzman's school watching Tino spar with the Black Belts. Tino called me over and introduced him as his "cousin." I sat next to Tiny and we watched Tino go through some of his Kenpo techniques with the other students. It was the first time Tiny shared Lima Lama self-defense principles and techniques. He told me that he was teaching at his own school in the city of Huntington Park. Tiny said he owned that school with business partner Ralph Shun. He added that he was training in Kung-Fu with Ralph Shun and had formally studied Kung-Fu under Grandmaster Ark Wong. Tiny was one of original five members of the Lima Lama organization. More specifically, he was the *first* member of Tino's organization. I was so intrigued with Tiny's explanations of Kung-Fu and Lima Lama that I scheduled a visit to his school. Back then; Tiny called his style "Fighting Lima Lama". After a couple of visits I was hooked and joined Tiny's school. At the Huntington school I would often watch Tino visit and teach Tiny. Later I would travel to Diamond Bar. This was an opportunity, which became a blessing as I got to know Tino's family at an early age. While studying at his house I met Tino's father. I was amazed to see how well Tino's dad performed the entry blocks from the cross sets. When I asked if Tino learned Lima Lama from his father, Tino responded, "No, no, the other way around! I taught my dad the cross set movements, and (then I) taught Tiny." Tino then mention to me that at an early age he had learned from his dad and his uncle certain fighting techniques. Tino said, "It's very common for Samoans to play with sticks and knifes and of course hand to hand fighting came very natural to us. But it's not Lima Lama, that is my own creation."

The training continued through the evening. As Tino taught Tiny new Lima Lama movements, I tried to absorb everything. I would often see first- generation students come for training. It was there that I met Solomon Kaihewalu and John Louis. Later I met second-generation students Larry Mauga, George Malifua, Don Lombardo, Ted Tabura, and Rigo Lopez, to name a few. What I didn't understand was that my training was never with the other Black Belts students; I was always alone with Tino.

I once asked Tino, *"Why am I being taught alone and not with the other older Black Belt students?"*

*"I want to keep you out of the politics,"* Tino responded.

I didn't understand it at the time, but Tino was protecting me from outside influences that would interfere with my focus. He wanted me to concentrate on learning Lima Lama, not on the organizations inner squabbles. Taking such approach was exclusively Tino's choice. I was being taught Lima Lama in its purest form. I look back now and realize his approach was truly a blessing.

After 18 months of intense training, Tino, Tiny and Ralph Shun awarded me the rank of Black Belt in the arts of Lima Lama, Kung-Fu, Five Animal Style and the Mok Ga Style. The same honor was bestowed upon my classmate, Gary Knutson. We were proud to be the first Black Belt students in Lima Lama and Kung-fu of the Huntington Park School.

# 1968 Al Garza at Tiny's Lefiti's School in Huntington Park

**Promoted to First Degree Black from Tino, Tiny and Ralph Shun**

I eventually left Tiny's school and become a full-time student of Tino's. This was during my teenage years. I will always be extremely grateful for the knowledge Tiny imparted to me. In February 1973 Tiny Lefiti died of a heart attack. He was 43.

**Ted Tabura**
**A Great Lima Lama Martial Artist**
Ted Tabura earned his Black Belt in Okinawa-Te Karate and Lima Lama under John Louis. Thereafter, Ted became Tino Tuiolosega's second gereration student. Although Ted never became a member of

the original organization, he remained a devoted follower, student and representative of Tino Tuiolosega. Well liked, admired and respected, Ted was known for the fantastic Japanese sickle demonstrations.

Japanese for sickle, the "*Kama*" was a favorite exhibition weapon among gi-style martial artists. Ted's demos were not only entertaining, but also impressive. He often would perform to music to excite the crowd. Ted was a Kama master, twirling the sharp and dangerous weapon at lightning speed. At his very core lay a martial artist with a deep understanding of the weapon and the martial arts movements it represents.

His slicing and circular motions were things of beauty. Tabura was ever the showman; he loved the audience as much as the audience loved him. Ted carried on John Louis and Tino Tuiolosega's legacy by organizing the Festival of Kings Annual Karate Tournament in Hawaii. The Festival was a true martial arts exhibition and competition that honored the contributions of his Hawaiian martial arts ancestors. We all lost a friend and incredible technician when Ted died in 2013.

My student, Frank Juarez and I attended Ted Tabura's memorial service and funeral. It was no surprise that he was well liked and well respected throughout the martial arts community. Ted was a devoted Christian and Born Again believer who proclaimed his love for the Lord Jesus Christ to the end.

Tabura remained a proud practitioner of Lima Lama and always represented Tino Tuiolosega's style with integrity and appreciation. John Louis showed his vision when he selected his first teacher Grandmaster Gordon Doversola, but later continued his quest by mentoring Solomon Kaihewalu and Ted Tabura. While they hailed from different styles, these gentlemen shared one thing in common: They appreciated the wisdom, talent, and genius of Grandmaster Tino Tuiolosega.

# Chapter 21
## Recording History In Cerritos, CA

I began studying video production at nearby Pasadena City College. Since I was also studying Lima Lama from Mr. Tino, I decided to combine my two loves and film him and Lima Lama instructors. At first, Tino would not allow anyone to film him. However, for reasons I never knew he allowed me to videotape him at demonstrations. There was always a "no video recording allowed" announcement during his demonstrations. If Tino saw someone with a video camera, he would send one of his students to either put away their camera or confiscate their tape. My first video shooting occurred at a hospital in Cerritos, CA, and featured a special demonstration for Richard Nunez's son, who was suffering from polio. This performance took place in the early 1970s and I shot Super-8 film. I was fortunate to shoot all five members of the Lima Lama organization—Grandmaster Tino, John Louis, Tiny Lefiti, Sal Esquivel, Richard Nunez and Solomon Kaihewalu. Tino made sure no one else filmed the demonstration. That day I had four reels of Super-8 film. Tino performed the first few techniques with Sal Esquivel and after demonstrating individually with the other students, he unveiled something never before seen: he had all four students attack him simultaneously with hand strikes. The bad news is that I accidentally missed filming it. I mixed up the new film with the used and lost valuable footage. It is a mistake I have always regretted. I did, however, manage to record half hour of amazing Tino movements.

# Chapter 22
## Mexico's First Black Belt

Tino's first Latin student, Rigoberto Lopez, introduced Lima Lama to Mexico when he opened his first school in Tijuana in the mid-1970s. His students would later spread Lima Lama throughout Central America and the world. Some of his most-notable students included Fernando Castellanos, Jose Oliveros, Nibardo Sanchez, Jorge Vazquez, Mario Villanueva and Dan Mitchel.

Tino introduced me to Rigo Lopez in at his residence in Diamond Bar. Like Sal, Rigo had a background in competitive bodybuilding. In fact, the 5-foot-7 inch athlete finished third in the "Mr. Baja California" competition in Mexico in 1967. It is important to mention that long before Rigo began his Lima Lama education under Tino Tuiolosega, he already had a long martial arts history, including: Judo in 1957, Jiu-Jitsu in 1963, Okinawa Shoryin-Ryu in 1964 and Kung-Fu in 1968. This high level of proficiency allowed Rigo to see the worthiness in Tino's Lima Lama.

Rigo was warm and friendly, a gentleman off the mat and a fierce competitor on the floor. Rigo officially became Tino's student in 1966 then trained with him twice a week in Diamond Bar. For more than a year, Rigo traveled from his hometown of Tijuana to study with Tino. The trip took three hours by car (on a good day) and five hours by bus. This kind of commitment was unusual, but many students made similar sacrifices to train with Tino. I learned that in the mid-1960s, Rigo was trained in Karate and quite often would travel from Mexico to California to compete in point tournaments. That's when he first met Sal Esquivel and the two soon became friends. Sal and Richard Nunez joined forces and gave Lima Lama Seminars in Mexico. Sal introduced Rigo to Tino and he officially became Tino's student. Tino then began a long and quite successful association with Mexico, giving seminars and promoting the Lima Lama Organization.

**GM Rigo Lopez**

**Tijuana, Mexico Demonstration At "La Plaza De Toros"**

One of Tino's first public demonstrations took place in Tijuana's bull-fighting ring arena known as "La Plaza de Toros". It is pretty odd for a Karate event to place at a bull-fighting ring, especially considering that most gi-related events are held in sports arenas or college gyms. Bulls died here; people lost their lives here. To the citizens of Mexico, holding a Karate tournament in a bull-fighting arena was not only natural, but also accepted.

During intermission, Tino was introduced to the audience as the Grandmaster of Lima Lama. He walked confidently up the stage and straight to the center of the arena. In tow was his entourage. This was no ordinary entourage; it was composed of Rigo's top Black Belt assistants. Nobody expected these assistants to launch at full-force, no-holds-barred attack at Tino. The performance began with the assistants offering the Lima Lama salutation first to Grandmaster Tino and then to the audience.

These assistants broke the relative calm by attacking their Grandmaster. Grandmaster Tino executed his movements with lightning speed and power, sending the attackers crashing to the ground one by one. The arena crowd was stunned by the feat of strength and power. Puzzled by the reaction, or lack of it, Tino turned his head to survey the crowd. Just as quickly, silence turned to bedlam as the crowd rose in unison and cheered so loud the walls of the venerable arena seemed to shake. People rushed from their seats and flowed to the arena floor, just to shake hands with the Grandmaster. It was almost surreal. It was at that moment that Tino became a martial arts folk hero.

Only later did Tino admit that he was concerned about seeing so many people coming toward him. Since he wasn't sure whether the crowd was there to bury or praise him, he assumed a fighting stance. But as they got closer he could tell that they just wanted to congratulate him. Tino relaxed and enjoyed the admiration. It was an extraordinary and unforgettable moment in time.

# Chapter 23
## Hurdles In Mexico

Any fledgling organization is bound to face its share of obstacles. Maybe it's a lack of economic resources; or bad management; or no direction; or poor communication. This translated into misunderstandings among its members that led to hurt feelings and unavoidable disappointment. This kind of turmoil often happens within small groups or families. For Lima Lama, Mexico was no different. This doesn't mean the members south of the border were purposely trying to sabotage the style. Rather, they just had different ways of trying to achieve the end result. The root of the problem centered on the responsibilities of its members. Roles were not clearly defined so there was no hierarchy. No one was in charge because everyone thought he was in charge. Subsequently, some members tired of the politics grew discouraged and chose to go out on their own. Rigo was among the group of practitioners who eventually separated from the Lima Lama organization. Born was Kung Do-Lama.

When I visited Rigo at his school in Tijuana, Mexico, he emphasized an utmost respect for Lima Lama, Tino Tuiolosega, and his former Lima Lama peers. Rigo promised to always support Tino and his organization's goals, because Tino was like a father to him. When Rigo stayed at Tino's Diamond Bar home, he developed a beautiful friendship with Tino, his family and the Lima Lama group. That feeling never wavered, even through Lima Lama's internal strife. Rigo admitted that he thought the language barrier ultimately led to the breakdown. Rigo did not speak English and Tino did not speak Spanish, making it difficult at times to discuss ideas or clarify matters of importance. This was in stark contrast to the study and teaching of Lima Lama. Since Tino "taught by example," the movements were simple to understand and easy to follow. Tino demonstrated Lima Lama movements and his students followed the examples. While Rigo acknowledges that there may have been a few instances when he needed translation with the physical side of Lima Lama, he maintains following Tino's step-by-step techniques was the best education a student could get. Sadly, the administration of the organization was often lost in translation. That being said, it is a pretty good bet Rigo would have gone his own way regardless of the internal problems. He had a great martial arts background before entering Lima Lama and studying with Tino only made his techniques faster, sharper and more powerful. It was in his martial arts DNA to experiment. Yet, he always proclaimed his allegiance to Tino and Lima Lama.

## The Growth of Lima Lama in Mexico

By the mid-1970s, Lima Lama was spreading beyond the border of Tijuana, Mexico. The man most responsible for this is Jorge Vasquez Ceballos, whose linage can be traced to Master Rigo Lopez, Mexico's first Black Belt under Tino Tuiolosega. Rigo Lopez' work with Jorge paid off when the student carried the "torch" of Lima Lama from Tijuana to Mexico City. Grandmaster Ceballos helped

Lima Lama matriculate to South and Central America. He even traveled to Spain to share Lima Lama with the Europeans.

# Chapter 24
## Westminster School
### 1972-1978

Tino's first commercial martial arts school was the Westminster Lima Lama School in Orange County, CA. Before Westminster, Tino lived in Diamond Bar but taught seminars throughout Southern California. It all changed with the opening of the Westminster studio and a partnership with Futi Semano, a fellow Samoan.

I met Futi when he joined a group of students attending Tiny's Huntington Park Lima Lama. Futi earned a Black Belt under Tiny and with it an introduction to Tino.

I continued to train with Tino during the early years of the Westminster School. Even though the trip to Westminster was longer, it was well worth the extra time. However, I took a break from studying to serve in the United States Coast Guard. While I was gone, Tino was not only teaching his Lima Lama students, but also his three sons—Rudy, Myron, and Kaipo. Rudy Tuiolosega was a success on the national competition circuit, finishing first or second most of the time. Rudy eventually was promoted to the rank of "*Malamalama*" or Senior Master 10-degree Black Belt in 2004 at Jeff Speakman's International Training Camp in Las Vegas. Myron and Kaipo continued their Lima Lama studies under their father and each received high-ranking Black Belts from Tino.

In 1971, after finishing my service with the Coast Guard, I returned to California and moved to Alhambra where I got married, went to college and opened a Lima Lama school in San Gabriel.

In 1975, I produced a cable television program called "*Martial Arts and Body Motions.*" One of my featured guests was Tino Tuiolosega. The television show included a 20-minute segment broken into interview and demonstration segments. Tino brought along sons Rudy and Myron, as well as students from the Westminster School. The students opened the show, Tino talked about history, philosophy and technique and finished with him demonstrating Lima Lama at the Grandmaster level. Having GM Tino as my guest made this martial art show one of my best segments I have done.

### Letter from Greg Spencer

I received a letter years later from a student who trained at the Westminster Lima Lama School. His name was Greg Spencer and he had received a Black Belt from Tino in the early 1970s. This is what he wrote:

*"The school opened in the early 1970s. I joined the Westminster Lima Lama School after meeting Rudy (Tino's son). During my first visit to the school, Fugi Semano (pronounce Fuki) was there. Fugi was first a Black Belt from Tiny Lefiti, was later introduced to Tino, and became his student and Black Belt.*

At the school Mr. Tino did most of the teaching. Among the Black Belts during my time were Tino's sons, Rudy, Myron, and Kaipo. The other Black Belts were Alan Dinsmore, Stan Johnson, Curtis and Darcy Adkins, a Samoan gentleman named Lata, Beau McDougall and Orlando Garcia.

I had known Alan, Curtis and Darcy most of my life and I brought them to the school. Curtis and Darcy Adkins were taking Tang So Do from the Alegria brothers. We all got our Black Belts from Mr. Tino. When the school closed, I would take classes and privates from Mr. Tino at his house in Fountain Valley, CA. Classes were held in the morning, as I was going to school and working. The classes were small, two-to-three people. Another student practitioner who trained in the Westminster school under Mr. Tino was a Japanese actor named Tadashi Yamashita. Tadashi was always watching the class. Rudy said he was training with his dad. I knew Yamashita from the show, "Thrill Seekers" where he did weapons demonstration blindfolded. I watched the Black Belts work out and was impressed. I also figured this might be is the right school, especially if Yamashita was training here. I don't know how Mr. Tino and Tadashi met, but they were good friends.

Yamashita came to class almost every night. He never worked out, just watched. After class, he would work on the techniques we learned. He would use Rudy, Myron and later me as punching bags. He was extremely fast. Tadashi incorporated the fluid hand techniques of Lima Lama into his martial arts system. You could *always find Lima Lama in his videos and magazine articles. People like Ed Parker and Tadashi Yamashita would show up at the house to rehearse fight scenes for a movie called, "Seven", in which they were main actors. The movie was released in 1979. It was an action film about a government agent who discovers a plot by a cartel of seven gangsters to take over Hawaii. He hires a team of seven hit men to stop them. Ed Parker was the main hit man and Mr. Tino played a gangster who had a bodyguard (Tadashi). I later encountered Mr. Tino in Hawaii (early 1990s). He was married to Adele and had a son, Joseph. At the time there was quite a Lima Lama following in Hawaii thanks to Master Steven Kupihea.*

*The Westminster school closed down in the late 1970s. Mr. Tino had graduated from law school and specialized in corporate contracts. A friend from law school offered him a job overseas. Tino took the job and decided to retire from Lima Lama.*

**GM Tino Tuiolosega  Co-Host Vernon Wells
Host Al Garza - World Of Martial Arts 1995
Aired On Cable TV**

**Practicing For The Movie 7 Tino Tuiolosega
Ed Parker – T.  Yamashita**

**In Hawaii- Greg Spencer- GM Tino- Steven Kupihea
Don Ghio-Joey Tuiolosega - Doug McLeod**

Tino went to Mexico in 1978 and announced his Lima Lama retirement. Since Rigo was retired, Mexico was without a leader.

# Chapter 25
## Tino In Europe 1979

### Back at the Stadium

*The Master is looking at a uniform hanging by the door. He is remembering how Tino left the Lima Lama Organization without saying good-bye to most of his Lima Lama practitioners.*

*"Why did Tino leave for 13 years?"* The Master wonders aloud.

*"It remains a mystery to me and others. How could Tino have just left?"*

*It was about this time that Tino and Claire separated. The divorce was later finalized when he returned from Europe.*

*"Nobody knew exactly where he went or why, he just left without saying good-bye to anyone,"* The Master explained.

*"Yes, he did go to Mexico and announce his retirement, but it was not like that in America. No retirement announcement to his friends; he just packed up and left."*

I can recall searching for Tino at his home, at his school, at his friends. I called his family but the phone had been disconnected. Even the family was gone. I couldn't find anyone to answer my questions. I eventually gave up and decided to move on with my teaching and life—until one day I found myself on an airplane heading toward Mexico to find Tino.

*The Master rises from his chair and walks toward the front door of his room. He thinks about his expedition to Mexico. "Ah yes, now I remember how my travel to Mexico started."*

During Tino's absence from Lima Lama, I learned that my friend Hector Ventura was searching for anyone who might know of Tino's whereabouts. His efforts paid off when he located Tino's son, Myron. Hector had originally met Myron through Lima Lama Master Ted Tabura. Hector convinced Myron to come to Mexico and teach Lima Lama under his father's name. Hector realized his goal of teaching Lima Lama in Mexico by also enlisting the help of Rudy Tuiolosega. It was through the family that Hector found Tino and convinced him to come out of retirement and continue teaching Lima Lama in Mexico. The 1990 reunion was pivotal, because it helped rekindle a relationship with Tino's family after 13 years.

After obtaining Myron Tuiolosega's phone number from Hector, I reconnected with Tino's family. Myron let me know the good news—that his father had left Europe and was teaching in Mexico. I felt both joy and relief; I knew that my friend and lifelong teacher was alive and well and on this side of the Atlantic. I hopped a plane with my son Albert and flew to Mexico City. Getting there was easy; finding him proved much more difficult.

# Chapter 26
## Searching for Tino in Mexico

Within a couple of days we were searching for Tino in Mexico City. Searching for my Grandmaster was an exciting endeavor. First, I was spending precious time with my eldest son. Secondly, I was confident in finding Tino—my friend and teacher—whom I had not seen in 13 years. We were detectives and we had a foolproof plan. I hired a taxi driver as a guide and pinpointed most of the Lima Lama schools in the city. Who better to know the location of their Grandmaster than Mexico City's Lima Lama Teachers?

It only took me a couple of days to discover my plan had major flaws. While I managed to contact numerous Lima Lama Schools, none had the slightest idea where Tino was staying. My confidence took a major hit and I gave up. As far as I was concerned, the search for Tino had come to an end. Still, there was something magical about the city so we decided to stay a couple of days longer.

We spent the next two days doing all the typical touristy things— visiting the Aztec Temples, the Teotihuacan Pyramids, the amazing church of La Villa de Guadalupe and gorgeous forest tree park, "Chapultepec", which dates back to the age when Maximiliano, Austria's Emperor Mexico, inhabited the palace of Chapultepec. The sightseeing was both educational and enjoyable. It was fascinating to learn how things were centuries ago in Mexico's main city, originally named Teotihuacan by the Aztecs. It also was a nice distraction from the disappointment of not finding Tino.

We were a bit tired from running around so we headed back to pack and prepare for our flight the next day. When we arrived at our hotel, we could hear a rather loud commotion across the street. I saw a large gathering of people crowded around someone. I looked at my son and wondered if it might be a famous movie star or politician.

*"Let's go over there and see what's going on,"* I said.

We quickly crossed the street, approached the crowd and were shocked when a black car pulled up. Waiting for the vehicle were four men sporting Lima Lama emblems on their shirts. The car door swung open and out climbed none other than Tino Tuiolosega, my teacher!

*"It's Tino, it's Tino, and he's here!"* I shouted at my son.

We both quickly ran inside the hotel to cut Tino off before he got in an elevator.

*"Tino,"* I yelled out toward him.

He turned and saw us standing there waving our hands at him. His entourage turned and wondered who we were. Tino recognized us at once. Without hesitation, Tino firmly walked over, hugged me tightly and asked, "What are you doing here?" My voice swelled with emotion.

*"I came looking for you. I haven't seen you in over 13 years and heard you were here in Mexico."*

Tino's eyes welled up with tears. He hugged me again and invited up to accompany him upstairs. It was a dream comes true. I looked straight into my son's eyes, smiled and nodded. I glanced at Albert.

*"We found Tino,"* we seemed to be saying to each other.

I can only say finding Tino was a miracle, the kind of miracle that reinforces one's faith in God. I can't explain how it happened. I can't explain what made us head back to the hotel at that very moment or why we crossed the street. It is best to accept miracles for what they are.

## Video Taping Our Interaction In Mexico City

When we stepped into Tino's room it was like a family reunion, only composed of a small group of students. The group included Tino, his student Ralph from Santa Cruz, CA, my son and I. We tried to catch up on lost time. First, I recounted how we "accidentally" found Tino in Mexico City after spending days searching for him. He was surprised to say the least. Is it Divine intervention or coincidence? At this moment it didn't really matter.

Traveling to Mexico City to find Tino impacted him deeply. He was touched by the loyalty I had for my teacher and friend. I know he valued our effort to find him. I told Tino that he had been missed in California and that people were concerned for his well-being. And then I admitted that my decision to find him turned out to be a true blessing. We chatted about our families and friends. I then took a shot and asked Tino if I could videotape him so his friends in California could see that he was okay. I also wondered if it was all right to record us discussing Lima Lama. He gave his approval and began the videotaping. I started to ask him questions about Lima Lama while I was thinking about how to do the interview. I wanted to keep the atmosphere loose so I started joking with him while he was answering questions. I let Tino know how the Lima Lama organization in the United States had changed in his absence. I also related that the five original members had created their own style and were teaching as Grandmasters. I told Tino that the pure Lima Lama system was never taught to anyone. Instead, the basic and the intermediate levels they were teaching were not part of his system.

*"From the beginning you have not taught Lima Lama systematically and that's why Lima Lama is being taught differently by each of your five original Black Belts,"* I told him. *"Lima Lama exists through you alone and only you taught advance techniques to your students and never the basic and intermediate levels of this Lima Lama system."*

I knew that I should not be saying these things, but I felt he needed know the truth. Tino looked at me and nodded. I could tell by the changing expression on his face he was upset with what I relayed to him.

*"Without a system, pure Lima Lama could not be practiced, shared, and spread in its purest form,"* I said.

Tino's face grew stern and serious. He was angry.

*"Garza, I don't teach system, don't worry about it!"* Then he changed the topic.

Clearing the air when it came to Lima Lama, Tino laid out his teaching approach and listed the Black Belts he personally recognized. He then shared the events that made him proud; the people that disappointed him; and the actions that touched his heart both positively and negatively. Tino was bearing his soul to me. The man who gained fame as a fierce fighter, the man whose mere gaze struck fear in the hearts of his opponents, was now the picture of sadness. The look was one of a father who had been let down by his children.

My son and I left for Acapulco the next day. However, we did not leave empty handed. We brought home something much more valuable than gold; we were treated to a real family reunion with my teacher, mentor, and lifelong friend. Tino marked history in the world of Lima Lama and I solved the mystery of my missing Grandmaster. The search for Tino was over! I thanked God for bringing us 2,000 miles south to find my close friend, teacher and mentor, the ultimate authority, the only founder and Grandmaster of Lima Lama, Tino Tuiolosega.

*As the Master stares out at the Stadium he can't help but think about his meeting with Tino.*

I remembered asking Tino to perform a short demonstration for my television show, "*The World of Martial Arts.*"

"*OK Al, just for you, I'll do it,*" he said.

He rose from his chair and told my son to stand up and assist him. My son, Albert, looked nervous as Tino instructed him to punch at him.

Tino then told Albert: "*I work simple; your dad knows this, so punch at me slow so I won't hurt you.*"

I proceeded to record his demonstration. He sent my son to the floor with so little effort one wondered if it was less martial art and more physics. I was thankful that Tino had given me his time (his demonstration). We then sat and discussed the future of his Lima Lama in America and Mexico.

*Back at the Stadium, the Master smiles and says to himself, "I can still see Tino there seated on his chair as we talked. It was a profound meeting between us. Yes, it was good to see my teacher again after so many years and I knew I would see him again. I can clearly see him as we said our good-byes. I was going to Acapulco and Tino was going back to the 'States."*

The meeting with Tino was both philosophical and spiritual. We talked about his art, his creation, his "Hands of Wisdom" Lima Lama and ultimately his spiritual values. From that day forward, I realized that in this capital city of Mexico, Tino was teaching fundamental Lima Lama techniques, just as he did in the United States. Nevertheless, those motions were not how Tino moved in his earlier years.

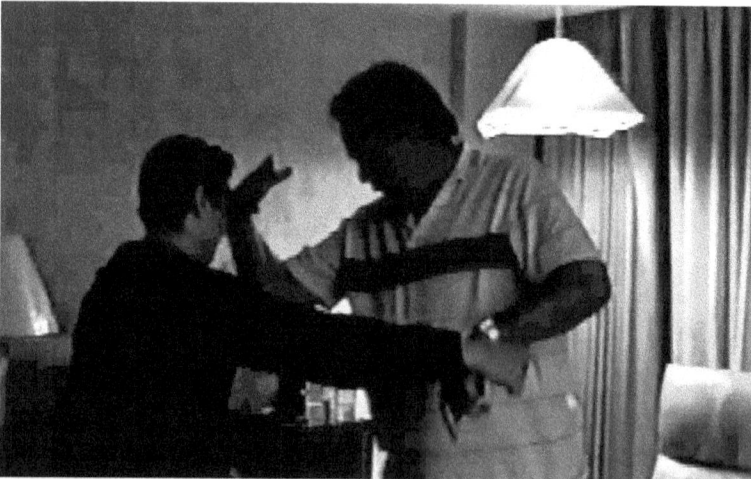

**Albert Garza II And GM Tino In Mexico City Acapulco, Mexico**

I went to Mexico City to see Mr. Tino. After our meeting at the hotel, he gave me his post office box address in Huntington Beach and told me to write to him there. The next day my son and I left Mexico City and moved on to the exotic and gorgeous port of Acapulco. After the family reunion with Tino, we found it easy to relax and enjoy the trip as a real vacation. We stayed at the Casablanca Hotel. We were simply exhausted and got what we needed most: rest. It was a marvelous trip, because there was peace and quiet in this tropical corner of Mexico. Acapulco was therapeutic and enjoyable. Later, we visited a few spots. Among these was La Quebrada, a high rocky cliff site where professional cliff divers jump from amazing heights into the ocean water below. This was a true show of courage, although other people might see this as clear evidence of insanity. However, I realized this is how these professional risk-taking divers making a living. The diving was spectacular and entertaining. Albert and I had a great time watching and enjoyed everything Acapulco had to offer.

As our week of rest and touring came to an end, I must say that Acapulco is beautiful. It has mystery, beauty, and of course, hospitality.

My son and I loved this place, but it was time to go home. We finally got back to Los Angeles. Within a few days we adjusted to our normal schedules and renewed our martial arts pursuit.

A month later I received a phone call from my good friend Don, one of Tino's and Richard Nunez' oldest Black Belts from the early days of Lima Lama. Don told me that he had contact with Tino and that he was in Santa Cruz, CA. He told me that a group of his old students were invited to come to Santa Cruz to celebrate Tino's birthday.

*"Can you make it Al, you're invited,"* Don asked.

*"Of course, I'm going and I'm bringing my son Albert with me,"* I answered.

# Chapter 27

## The Lima Lama Of Santa Cruz

It was July and Tino was celebrating his 60th birthday. Family and some of his earlier Lima Lama Black Belts would be his guests at the celebration. A meeting was also scheduled to take place. We drove to Santa Cruz and met Tino in the "Kenposilama School" where he was teaching. Kenposilama was a compilation of: "Ken" for Kenpo; "Sil" for Silum Kung-Fu; and "Lama" for Lima Lama. The school belonged to Dio and his wife Clara who were early students of Doug McLeod, a Kenpo Black Belt in Ed Parker's system.

Tino was now divorced and had a new family—a younger wife, Adele, and a new son, Joey. This came as quite a surprise since he never mentioned his new family to me in Mexico City. Nevertheless, Tino was happy and that in turn made me happy. Tino met Adele through his old Kenpo friend, Doug McLeod. She was a beginning student at McLeod's Kenpo Karate School in Santa Cruz. At one time she was a professional travel photographer for a private company. Of Italian descent, Adele's family had settled in Santa Cruz. Joey was 14 when I met him and he was already a Black Belt in Kenposilama. I could see that his hands were very quick. We became good friends and often on our free time we would play rock, paper and scissors. Most of our games came out even, but I must say, I was the last winner (sorry Joey)

**GM Tino Tuiolosega   Al Garza   Joey Tuiolosega**

**Courtesy Picture by Adele Tuiolosega**

## Adele And GM Tino In Tokyo Japan

During my stay in Santa Cruz, I got a chance to know and appreciate Adele. In time we became good friends. She was very nurturing and you could tell she really loved Tino. Tino truly loved her and appreciated her as well

Later in the afternoon, I met Tino's other sons from his first wife, Claire: Myron, Rudy, and Kaipo. At the school, I also met Bill, his highest-ranking Black Belt from Santa Cruz. The other Black Belts there were Don, Ralph, Gilbert, my son Albert, little Joey, Dio, Big John and Clara. Others were present but I never knew their names. We gathered at the school, and then Tino took us to his home a few blocks away. Tino explained that he had settled in Santa Cruz 10 Years earlier after retiring following a tour of Europe.

His 60th birthday celebration was a chance to reunite with close friends and family. He announced that he was ending his Lima Lama retirement and wanted us to be part of his new organization. Tino said that during training the next day he would show us his new style of Lima Lama. I shared with Tino that I was still producing my own martial arts TV show. My half-hour program featured different martial artists and styles. I followed with my request: would it be OK for me to videotape the workout and make it part of my martial arts show. Tino agreed with my request.

After the meeting, we all went back to our hotels and prepared for Tino's birthday celebration. We met at a nearby Chinese restaurant that evening had dinner and capped off the night by singing "Happy Birthday." The food was delicious and we all enjoyed his birthday cake to the fullest. Tino and Adele left early that evening, while the rest of us just relaxed and caught up on old times. This was truly an unforgettable occasion.

**Picture taken in Santa Cruz, California**

**1993 GM Tino And Sons  Rudy, Myron, Kaipo and Joey**

## The Santa Cruz Lima Lama (In the Morning)

The next day we headed to the "Kenposilama School" where Tino had put together a program. We were so excited to see Tino, his family and the extended Lima Lama family we hardly paid attention to the appearance of the "Kenposilama" School. However, this morning we noticed that the Kenposilama School was a martial arts studio in every sense of the word. It was a professional, spacious and active training location, replete with mirrors, a heavy bag, and students donning black uniforms. Noticeably absent were Lima Lama patches on their gis. Instead, the emblem featured the "Kenposilama School." This was surprising to us all. After exchanging greetings, Tino asked me to grab my camera and take video of Bill, Raphael, Dio and Clara going through the basics. He then instructed the guys to sit and watch as I recorded his Kenposilama students' training session. I recorded over two hours of his latest techniques and forms that day. Then it was time for our training—four hours of continues movements.

By the time we were done with the morning session, we were tired, thirsty, and hungry, so Tino gave us a break. Most of the guys showed signs of being a little confused with the new techniques. So when break time came along, the guys from Los Angeles went to have lunch. We continued to catch up on our lives, family, and work. There was plenty of talking, joking, laughing, and sharing, before the tone grew a little more serious when the subject of Lima Lama came up. Ultimately, the guys talked about what they had learned that morning at the Kenposilama School. The consensus was that the new

Lima Lama movements, techniques and forms were very different from what had been taught and practiced for so many years. Most of the LA guys admitted they were less than comfortable with the new direction. Tino's latest version hardly resembled the style they fell in love with a decade earlier. Even more discouraging was that these Lima Lama Black Belts felt like beginners. I understood and respected their opinions. These high-ranking martial artists spent a great portion of their lives learning and refining techniques, only to be told they needed to change their fighting stances, punches, blocks, kicks, forms and sparring technique.

I was more receptive to the "element of change" because Tino made "change" an integral part of my Lima Lama lessons. The other Black Belts weren't as fortunate; it was not part of their daily regimen. I agreed with their reservations, because now they were being told what they had been taught before was no longer valid. While it may be true that the only constant in life is change, the Los Angeles contingent was not about to turn their backs on years of martial arts accomplishment. They tried to incorporate the new Lima Lama in their regimen out of respect for their Grandmaster, but they found the transition too difficult. These guys truly respected and admired Tino, so it must have been hard for them to turn their backs on his new curriculum.

The original Lima Lama had style, speed, hand combinations, power, wrist movements, and wide stances, straight punches to the chest and the sparring perfect for point-fighting tournaments. In his

Santa Cruz Lima Lama, the stances took on the style of the boxer; his punches were now more versatile and his kicks were limited (no high kicks) for practical self-defense. He did this on purpose: He wanted a style for the streets, something simpler and more practical. To say which Lima Lama is better would be unfair. Tino Tuiolosega created both versions. Another difference is that Tino put his Santa Cruz Lima Lama style into a book, complete with pictures and videos. Also included were books for Lima Lama instructors and students. While I was in Santa Cruz I vowed to learn the new system. That's what Tino wanted his system to be. I learned by watching the way he moved, his body alignment and his hand position after each block or strike. It was so different from what had been taught before. I learned what I could during my stay there and videotaped his new Lima Lama during the workouts and seminars.

After one of our workouts Tino stopped by my hotel later that night to see how I was doing. We talked about what I was teaching, his return to martial arts and what his plans were for his Lima Lama arts of self-defense.

# Chapter 28
## The Next Visit to Santa Cruz

A year later, during one of my visits to Tino's home in Santa Cruz, my son and I were introduced to a group of men from Spain. It was late 1993 and Tino had invited the Spaniards to stay with him and train at his house. They stayed in Santa Cruz for six months and trained at the Kenposilama School with Tino and his Black Belts. I was impressed with their determination, devotion, good character and friendliness.

Spains introduction to Lima Lama started with Carlos Becerra who first started learning Lima Lama under the direction of Jorge Vazquez. He was later joined by Juan F. Freire Fernandez, Alfonso Guerrero, Felipe Cachón, and Jose Gómez.

It was Jorge Vazquez that introduced them to Tino. At first Carlos and a few of his students later came to Santa Cruz to stay for a month. They promised to return the following year and learn his Lima Lama system. In a strange twist, they also vowed not to cut their hair until they had returned to Santa Cruz and learned Lima Lama. And so it was, when I first met these Spaniards they all had hair down to their shoulders.

Being with the guys visiting from Spain and sharing different ideas turned out to be a rewarding experience. The guys were attentive and respectful. We all enjoyed spending time with Tino, his family, his students and friends at the practices and at our gatherings. During the final afternoon of our Santa Cruz break, Tino stopped by the hotel to chat. We discussed the old Lima Lama and what he was presently teaching in Santa Cruz. Tino's wishes were to have Lima Lama taught all over the world in a standardized manner. That's why he wrote the instructional book and produced the accompanying video.

*"Yes, by all means yes,"* I answered, promising to incorporate the program into my teaching curriculum.

I then asked Tino if he would like to see the Lima Lama fundamentals I was teaching my students.

*"Yes, I'd like that Al,"* he said, sitting back in his chair.

I explained to Tino that these were my 20 basic defensive entries or the first defensive block and strike to an opponent's attack. I then demonstrated the movements. I finished, looking for approval. Instead, he stood up, looked me square in the eyes and said,

*"Al, don't teach that, I don't want you to teach that anymore."*

"*Why,*" I asked him, more than a bit confused.

"*You don't know what you have, these movements are far to advanced. You shouldn't be teaching that!*"

"*I'm sorry Tino. I've been teaching these basics since you left the country 13 years ago and I can't stop now.*"

I tried to be careful with my comments.

"*Tino, I understand what you're saying. I know what it represents when I teach this. I know it's an advanced fighting system that I'm teaching and not techniques, but this is what I teach.*"

That answer did not please Tino. He nodded and simply said. "OK." And that was it. End of conversation. After that, we changed the subject, touching on his family, his days in Europe and today's version of Lima Lama.

I returned to Los Angeles and continued teaching, but this time I included some of Tino's basic Lima Lama curriculum. In 1995, Tino asked me to join him on his trip to Spain. His family and student, Raphael, also would be going on the three-week seminar tour. Tino wanted me to videotape everything and air it on my martial arts television show.

This trip to Spain was a great opportunity as I was producing a TV cable program. I could make our trip the first martial arts reality show.

**Tino's Heart Attack and Stroke**

I made frequent trips to Santa Cruz to study with Tino before going to Spain. In 1994, shortly after one of my Santa Cruz trips, I was home in Los Angeles when I received a phone call from Adele. She told me that Tino had suffered another heart attack and was in the hospital. She related that Tino would need a heart bypass and that he was scheduled for it the next day. I told Adele I would keep Tino in my prayers and asked if she would let me know how the operation went. I let her know I would go see Tino as soon as he was able to accept visitors. Adele called me a few days later and told me the bypass went as planned, but that during the operation Tino had suffered a stroke. He had lost his ability to talk, use his right hand and right leg. Doctors said he would need speech and physical therapy. About a month later I drove to Santa Cruz with Hector Ventura and immediately went to the hospital to see Tino. We weren't allowed to stay long. So we expressed our care as we stayed there a few days and then left for Los Angeles.

I returned a few months later and while Tino was walking; all he could do was drag his leg when he walked. Since he was unable to talk, he was learning to express himself through hand signs and writing with his left hand.

Even after the bypass and stroke, the trip to Spain remained on the agenda. Adele called me and asked me if I was still interested in accompanying Tino and the family to Spain. I was overjoyed that he still wanted me with him. The footage I took from that trip turned into one of the best shows ever produced on Lima Lama.

# Chapter 29

## California to Spain

We arrived in Madrid and naturally felt stiff from 14 hours on the plane. But we couldn't wait to explore this beautiful Spanish city. We were greeted at the airport by Tino's students Juan Fernandez, Alfonso Guerrero, Felipe Chacon, Jose Gomez and Carlos Becerra. We arrived at a house outside Madrid that belonged to a Lima Lama student. We would be staying in a small town about 30 minutes from the city. After a few days of jet lag our bodies adjusted and we were ready to go.

One evening, we visited Carlos Becerra's school and Tino did a short demonstration with Rafael. Tino's demonstration was simple and sweet. He was still full of surprises, despite only being able to demonstrate mostly with his left hand. Nevertheless, he showed determination and confidence as he flowed through his techniques. Rafael then took over and taught techniques from Santa Cruz.

Most days were spent sightseeing in Madrid. We visited many parts of the city, including historic churches, the Prado National Museum, the Plaza Mayor and the Royal Palace. It truly captured our imagination. One day we took a trip to the city of Toledo, which is about a two-hour drive from Madrid. Once the capital of Spain, Toledo still retains the atmosphere, charisma and enchantment for which so many European cities are famous. Toledo is a spectacular city, its rustic buildings and winding streets holding hundreds of years of history.

In one of my videos, you can see students from Spain demonstrating their Lima Lama techniques while Grandmaster Tino is standing next to the River Tajo. The historic Alcazar Castle is in the background. It was extraordinary to see Tino Tuiolosega share his Lima Lama with the Spaniards and the world.

After a week in Madrid, we flew to Barcelona, where we stayed at a beachfront hotel and visited several Lima Lama schools. Rafael conducted the seminars under the direction and supervision of Grandmaster Tino. After the seminars and a day of rest, we were invited to attend a Barcelona Lima Lama tournament. Tino was the guest of honor and he appeared in front of hundreds of spectators. His entrance was grand. Led into the gymnasium by an entourage of Black Belt students, Tino stopped and offered a Lima Lama Salutation to the audience. He proceeded to the middle of the gymnasium, called Rafael and performed techniques. The audience was enthralled. Rafael and Joey followed with a demonstration of techniques from Santa Cruz. The crowd showed their appreciation with a lengthy standing ovation. Tino's face was beaming.

The three weeks we spent in Spain were truly historical. The visit filled our minds with memories and our hearts with appreciation for the reception we received. It was truly a dream come true for Tino and his family, Rafael and myself.

Madrid     Barcelona    Toledo Spain

Courtesy Picture by Adele Tuiolosega

# Chapter 30
## American Samoa, 1996

Six months after our Spain trip while I was visiting Tino in Santa Cruz, Adele invited me to go with them to Samoa. She told me that Tino was going home to Pago Pago to visit his mom. She also wanted her son Joey to meet Tino's mom, his grandmother and other family relatives living in Samoa. I said I would love to go and videotape it.

Pago Pago is where Tino was raised and received his early education. It was also here that Tino learned to streetfight and earned a dubious reputation within the community. I must admit, the flight from Hawaii to Pago Pago shook me up a bit. Our commercial airplane looked more like a "puddle jumper" with a 40-seat capacity. And just as we were about to land, a thunderstorm hit. We could see lightning from our windows. Adele, Joey, and I were more than a bit nervous as we gripped our arm rests with passion. Tino, on the other hand, was quite calm, almost as if he'd made this journey thousands of time. As we began our descent, I could see lightning illuminating what looked to be a small covered patio. I also spied that the airport's runway ended at the ocean. Our fears proved to be unfounded as we landed and then ran into a small building where our luggage was being inspected.

It seemed like we had just gone back in time: The people inside wore Hawaiian-flowered prints and straw hats. It was just like a scene from a 1940s movie. This was so different from Hawaii, which featured mixed races. Native Samoans occupied the landscape here.

Once inside the airport, we were greeted by Tino's stepbrother Trevor and Tino's son, Eric. Since we were staying for two weeks, I had the chance to meet Tino's mother, his stepsisters and stepbrothers. I sensed the love and warmth they felt for him. It had been years since he'd been back so they we eager to hear about his life. During the second week I had the opportunity to speak with Tino's family about what he was like growing up. I was told that Tino was very popular with the girls (as always) and that he was always getting in trouble in school. He loved to fight and he also loved the ocean.

Claire told me one reason the family sent Tino to live with one of their relatives in Hawaii was because he was always getting into fights and he was not taking his education seriously.

Our two weeks in Pago Pago was a true adventure. We had stayed at Eric's home during our two-week trip. He lived in a three-story home on top of a mountain; it was quite modern and very beautiful. In the morning I would go to the balcony and see the sun rise over the ocean. From his balcony I could see the airport by the ocean and from the other side of the house I could see the city (Pago Pago).

It was an incredible two-week journey. We traveled to all four points of the Island and visited different villages. The roads near the city were paved, but as we drove further from civilization asphalt turned to dirt. The homes in American Samoa were modern, but to my surprise, next to each home was a large modern-looking hut that resembled large patios with no walls. The supporting post was composed of either wood or bamboo material with mosquito nets draped from a pointed roof. Tino's brother told me those areas were reserved for family members to stay when they visited.

Both amusing and touching was that the family asked me to stay with them after Tino left. They said they could find me a good wife, since I was single at the time. I thanked them for their offer, but told them I would be returning to the Mainland. Touched by their kindness, I vowed to someday return.

Toward the end of our stay in American Samoa, we visited a courthouse where the photos of past and present judges hang on the wall. Tino pointed to one particular judge. It was a picture of his father, who had been a judge for a number of years and was part of Samoan history. Tears fell from Tino's eyes as he stared at the photo. The love he had for his dad was overpowering and touched us all. We left for California later in the week, carrying with us the kind of warmth and generosity that sticks with you for a lifetime.

**In Samoa GM Tino and his dad Judge Tuiolosega**

**Picture from the World of Martial Arts Program**

## American Samoa an Unincorporated U.S. Territory

American Samoa is a United States territory. It consists of small islands, of which Tutuila is the largest. The population in Tutuila (known as Pago Pago) is about 25,000 that live in small villages throughout the island. Considered its capital and main harbor, Pago Pago is a mixture of semi-urban communities, small towns and tuna canneries that provide work for one-third of the population.

*At the Stadium The Master thinks back to when he spoke to Claire about Tino's father.*

Claire told me that when his father died, she and Tino went to American Samoa to attend the funeral. When they reached Pago Pago, a special government ship was waiting to take them to the Island of Olosega.

*"Albert, I never thought he was that important,"* she related.

*"We were escorted by a government ship and taken to his Island. I was so impressed. When we got to Olosega, the people there greeted us and I was put on a flat platform and lifted up and carried by two men so I wouldn't have to touch the water. Then, both Tino and I were carried to the village.*

*Then we met all the family there. The head chiefs from all the villages came and brought us food. Later that evening, before the funeral, we were placed in a room and you'll never guess what was under the bed. I tell you, I never seen anything like this before. Under the bed were skeleton bones of Tino's ancestors. It's true, we were on top of his ancestors, and we slept there. Wow! It was amazing.*

*Then at the funeral, they placed his dad on top of a platform so all the people could come and give their respects. Throughout the day, before they buried him, the Chiefs from the villages would stand in front of the platform and yell out in their language, 'Here lays one of our Chiefs, the great Tuiolosega.' They would yell it from one village to another. It would be said from one Chief in the village to another Chief from a different village, back and forth, all day. It was something else I tell you."*

That was my only video interview with Claire Tuiolosega. She did it just for me and for my martial arts program. I thanked her for that evening and I left with much respect for her kindness.

# Chapter 31

# Cancun Mexico

In 1996, a year after our trip to Spain, I received another call from Adele. This time she asked me if I wanted to videotape their trip to Cancun for my television show. I said that I would be happy to join them again on this tour. This was Tino's first trip to Cancun, one of the southern-most regions in Mexico. Tino still could not speak, nor could he use his right hand or leg. But that was not about to stop him from experiencing life and spreading Lima Lama. He was teaching us a lesson much greater than any Lima Lama technique. He was teaching us about perseverance. His Lima Lama was being manifested through his courage and character. This was Lima Lama in its purest form. Disappointment turned into hope, into faith and I could not help but witness Tino's amazing fortitude.

We were hosted in Cancun by Nibardo Sanchez, one of Rigo Lopez' Black Belts from the Lima Lama School in Tijuana. I met Sanchez way back in the late 1960s when I was just 19. I had accompanied Tino to the border town of Tijuana, Mexico, to compete in a tournament. His Lima Lama teacher, Rigo Lopez, introduced me to Nibardo. It was just a quick hello. I lost touch with Sanchez until now in Cancun. Tino was visiting Cancun as a special guest to observe Nibardo's yearly belt promotion and celebrate the Lima Lama school grand opening. During our one-week stay in Cancun, Mr. Nibardo showed us the sights that make Cancun such a magical place. Mr. Nibardo went out of his way to make sure we experienced the beauty of this Mexican paradise. We first went to Tulum to see the Mayan Temple, also referred as El Castillo, with the whole setting surrounded by the gorgeous Mexican Caribbean coastline. While at the Temple, I asked Tino if he could do a short demonstration for my martial art show. And so in the midst of this magnificent site, Tino rose and flowed through Lima Lama. I realized that Tino was not here to perform. It was enough that he found the strength to make the trip.

This was the same man who had studied and excelled under Grandmaster Ed Parker, Grandmaster Ark Wong and other Chinese Grandmasters. This was the same martial artist who conceived and cataloged Lima Lama. Yet, even after heart surgery and a stroke, he was willing to share with the world his knowledge of Lima Lama. After Tino had treated us to his Lima Lama exhibition, Mr. Nibardo's Black Belts honored Tino with a Lima Lama demonstration for my camera.

We spent the rest of the day in Xel Ha, one of the largest Natural Aquariums in the world. We snorkeled with the fish, ate like kings at the restaurant and enjoyed the warmth and beauty of the aquarium. The next day we toured Cancun City, its shops, and the beach hotels. The following day we drove to the outskirts of Cancun and went to the beaches in Maya Rivera.

# Mr. Nibardo Sanchez And GM Tino Tuiolosega In Cancun Mexico

# Pictures From The World Of Martial Arts Program

## Mr. Nibardo Sanchez – Al Garza – GM Tino Tuiolosega

Mr. Nibardo Sanchez was the perfect host. He made sure we experienced the best Cancun had to offer. Tino appreciated Mr. Nibardo's kindness and hospitality during our tour of Cancun. After the day's events, we went back to the hotel to rest before the Lima Lama promotional event. Before we could fully recover from our tour of Cancun, we were dressed in our martial arts uniforms and attending the event. Mr. Nibardo promoted four of his brown belts to Black Belts. But the real surprise came when Grandmaster Tino Tuiolosega promoted Mr. Nibardo to $8^{th}$-degree Black Belt.

It's been 20 years since that trip but I still treasure my video of Tino demonstrating his Lima Lama techniques. I also have video of Mr. Nibardo and his students performing the original 12 techniques Rigo Lopez taught in his Lima Lama program. It was in Cancun that I saw what Nibardo Sanchez had learned from his teacher Mr. Rigoberto Lopez and Grandmaster Tino.

My memory of Tino in Cancun is unforgettable. It also reinforced my understanding of why Lima Lama was practiced differently. Mr. Nibardo expressed Lima Lama as Rigo had taught him. I valued and appreciated his hard work, and discipline. If Grandmaster Tino recognized their work, then we all should recognize each other's contribution and dedication. That was Tino's example.
I became friends with Mr. Nibardo during the Cancun adventure. Mr. Nibardo later came to California after Tino suffered another heart attack. Mr. Nibardo spent the next two years caring for Tino in his home and with the Lima Lama organization TILOA.

I got to know Mr. Nibardo better during his California stay with Tino. The more we talked, the better he understood my background and skills in Lima Lama. He also became aware of my many years of friendship with Tino. He was shocked to know that not only had I not been promoted for more than 20 years, but that I was ranked as a 3rd-degree Black Belt in Lima Lama.

This was due, in part, to Tino retiring from Lima Lama and then disappearing. It was Mr. Nibardo who spoke to Tino about promoting me to $8^{th}$-degree Black Belt in Lima Lama. Mr. Nibardo told Tino that he knew I had been with him for many years and that I was an asset to his Lima Lama cause. Tino agreed and later that year promoted me to $8^{th}$-degree and Nibardo to $9^{th}$-degree Black Belt in Lima Lama. This was 1999, three years after my trip to Cancun, Mexico.

*At the Stadium With his hand on his chin, almost in a classic pose from "The Thinker", the Master reflects on his martial arts journey with Tino.*

# Chapter 32
## Tino's Lima Lama

I find it amazing that so many people today are teaching variations of Lima Lama so far removed from the original style. It's puzzling because no one has questioned why there is such a difference between the pure Lima Lama created by Tino and what is being offered by the world's instructors.

Tino's movements and his interpretation of those movements were the very essence of Lima Lama. The source of Lima Lama and its interpretation by generations of students continues to change as outside styles influence its core principles. It only goes to show that the more Lima Lama spreads throughout the world, the more it will adapt to the skills of martial artists from other styles. An example is the talented martial artist Nibardo Sanchez who developed and refined his interpretation of Lima Lama according to his teacher's perspective, Mr. Rigoberto Lopez, who is a great teacher with a diverse martial arts background.

In my videos I took of Tino in his early Lima Lama days shows a marked difference from how he demonstrated later in life. The film doesn't lie: you can see the changes Tino made to his Lima Lama and his method of execution. At the same time, one can observe Tino's students teaching from their perspective, their interpretation, and their growth in Lima Lama. The influence comes from each stylist's martial arts background.

Tino's understanding of Lima Lama was so far advanced his students had a hard time keeping up. He lived his life the way he practiced martial arts—with a never-ending passion for making each day more productive. Tino was this way from the time he arrived in Los Angeles and began studying with Ed Parker and Ark Y. Wong. As a result, he never had the time to teach the basics of Lima Lama. Instead, he taught only advanced multiple movements, which seemed to change from lesson to lesson. Ultimately, I recognized that it was impossible to emulate Tino. With no basics to draw from, it was only natural for new students to fall back on their core training in other styles. To make things worse, he failed to provide written material in those early years. Each student was left to his own memory. Consequently, a lot was left on the Dojo floor. It was only during his later years of teaching in Santa Cruz that Lima Lama was categorized and systematized through instructional manuals.

# Chapter 33
## The New Teaching Method


The more Nibardo and I became acquainted, the more time we shared our desire to see Tino succeed. I shared what I was teaching, including my formal written documents covering the entire progressive teaching curriculum. I was pleased to see Nibardo's openness with the teaching method I had developed. He liked that it was well structured and organized. I told him that the progressive system empowers a Lima Lama student to gradually develop and grow from level to level. My documents also spelled out the requirements from the white belt through the advanced master levels up to $9^{th}$-degree Black Belt. The curriculum also contained video of Tino performing his Lima Lama, as well as footage of his original Lima Lama students. Nibardo shared my progressive teaching curriculum with Tino, who agreed to think about adding it to his current program. Tino was not ready to make drastic changes. Instead, he wanted to concentrate on spreading his art in Mexico. He enlisted Nibardo's help in making that a reality. A year after Nibardo and I were promoted to higher Black Belt ranks, Nibardo traveled with Tino and his wife through Mexico, as well to other parts of the world.

After returning from Mexico Tino moved to the city of Huntington Beach, CA, I was summoned to a meeting with Nibardo, Tino and Adele. On the agenda was a discussion of my work in Lima Lama and the curriculum I had developed. At our gathering I formally presented my teaching curriculum. During our meeting, Nibardo told Tino that it would advance his Lima Lama by adding my teaching methodology to his existing curriculum. Tino nodded in agreement, and then Adele asked if I could make a copy of my work for them. While I was with Tino later that day, he played one of his Lima Lama videos. That footage showed one of his students teaching the fundamentals of his new Lima Lama. Tears streamed from Tino's eyes.

"*Why are you crying?*" He pointed to the television. "*Is that why you are crying?*" He nodded.

"*Well, that's your legacy*," I declared respectfully. "*It's what you've given your students.*"

I was trying to encourage Tino, as well as express my respect for his students. He looked at me and shook his head as if to say,

"*Yeah, I know, but I want more.*"

Tino then tapped me on the shoulder and pointed toward the door. He wanted to take a walk. As Tino and I went for a walk, he pointed to my folder, clearly indicating that he wanted to see my teaching documents again. We sat on a bench and Tino combed through the curriculum. He pointed his finger at me, then at the book in his hands.

"Yes," he said with an emphatic nod.

My lifelong friend, teacher and Grandmaster Tino made his intentions "clear" without ever saying a word. Just to make sure I understood, Tino gestured with his hands to confirm the requirements and Black Belt testing procedures.

*"Yes, I'll do this for you,"* I promised.

We went back inside and I replayed the moments Tino and I had just shared with Nibardo and Adele. I had committed myself to teach and share my progressive teaching method, by extending the old curriculum.

**This is the Letter Mrl Nibardo Sanchez sent to Al Garza.
Testifying to Mr. Garza's Progressive Teaching Method.**

En los años 1997 al 2000, su servidor Nibardo Sanchez; cinta negra 9º grado en Limalama, el gran master Tino Tuiolosega y la señora Adela iniciamos la organizacion de Tiloa en donde llegamos al acuerdo de proponer al master Al Garza como director tecnico de Tiloa y fue aceptado por la organizacion por su sistema Matrix para la enseñanza dentro del sistema Tiloa ya que este sistema de defensa personal es muy completo y efectivo. Cabe mencionar que para mi Al Garza siempre fue un gran amigo y un gran maestro de las artes marciales por la confianza que habia entre nosotros le segeri que esperara para tomar su cargo, que yo le avisaria cual seria el mejor momento para iniciar, pero surgieron ciertas anomalias dentro de la organizacion que tuve que tomar la decision de retirarme de la presidencia y en donde al mismo tiempo el master Al Garza tambien se retiro y no hubo la oportunidad de iniciar de nuevo este su sistema Matrix.

Desde entonces el mtro. Al decidio enseñar su sistema al publico de manera independiente y enfocado a maestros destacados de otros sistemas

Como maestro de Limalama al conocer el sistema Matrix no dude en recomendarle a mi hijo Nibardo Aram Sanchez Gonzalez siendo 5º grado en Lima Lima que aprendiera el sistema Matrix sin dejar nuestro arte Lima Lama.

Mtro. Nibardo Sanchez Osorio
Malamakoa

Letter from Mr. Nibardo Sanchez translated to English

*In the years 1997 thru 2000, Your Server Nibardo Sanchez Limalama 9<sup>th</sup> Degree Black Belt, The Grand Master Tino Tuiolosega, and The Grand Master's Wife Adele initiated the organization called; "TILOA", where we came to an agreement to tender Master Al Garza as Technical Director of TILOA and was accepted as well for by the organization because of his "Matrix System" to teach it as well within the "TILOA System" since this system of personal defense is very complete and effective. There is room to mention, that to me, Al Garza has always been a great friend and a great Master of Martial Arts. Because of the trust that there is between us, I suggested that he should wait to take the charge, that I would let him know when the best moment would be to initiate, but certain anomalies emerged within the organization that forced me to make the decision to retire from the presidency and at the same time Master Al Garza also retired; and there was no opportunity to initiate his Matrix System again.*

*Since then, Master Al decided on teaching his system to the public in an independent manner, while focusing on prominent masters from a variety of other systems.*

*As a LimaLama Master, once I got to know the Matrix System; I had no doubts in recommending My Son Nibardo Aram Sanchez Gonzalez being a Limalama 5<sup>th</sup> Degree Black Belt, to learn the Matrix System without leaving our Lima Lama.*

Master Nibardo Sanchez Osorio
Malamakoa

At the Stadium,

*The Master practices his techniques and prepares for his demonstration.*

I was pleased that Tino had agreed to use my progressive teaching method. Tino knew time was running out. He never fully recovered from his heart attack and stroke. He couldn't talk, couldn't walk well and struggled to teach. My progressive program made him once again think his Lima Lama objectives would be realized.

I know without a doubt in my heart the reason Tino revealed his sadness and permitted me to see him cry. He felt he was letting his students down, because he hadn't left enough for them to learn, progress, and grow to Lima Lama's purest form. What Tino saw in that video, what made him so melancholy, was the realization that there wasn't enough time to complete his Lima Lama journey. He saw it was his responsibility to prepare the next generation of Lima Lama practitioners. But as he viewed the video, he saw deficiencies in the advanced techniques, which could be attributable to inadequate basics. Since they only did what Tino instructed, he felt like a father who had let down his children. Still, Tino was overjoyed that someone had agreed to carry on the Lima Lama instruction.

It was during that time that I was named Executive Technical Director of the Tino Tuiolosega International Organization Association (TILOA). Nibardo would continue as President of

TILOA and, of course, Tino had a seat at the head of the Lima Lama Organization table.

I was excited to be part of Tino's team and appreciated everybody's acceptance. Approximately a year later, Tino's son, Rudy, returned to California and stayed with his dad in Huntington Beach. Rudy was enthusiastic about his dad's Lima Lama and expressed a desire to be involved in the organization. We were glad to have him join our team. I had known Rudy since he was a child and was sincerely happy to see him follow in his father's footsteps.

**Senior Master TILOA Lima lama Rudy Tuiolosega**

# Chapter 34

## Leaving the Lima Lama Organization

Rudy joined the team on the next trip to Mexico to help with the seminars and hand out promotions. However, during the visit Nibardo and Rudy started to disagree. Rudy was destined to become leader of the Lima Lama Organization, not only because he was Tino's son, but also because he was a talented martial artist. Nibardo understood how martial arts works, so as a sign of respect to Tino and his family, as well as Rudy, he reduced his level of participation in Tino's organization and returned to Cancun, Mexico. I am certain Nibardo was only recognizing Rudy's rightful position as a Tuiolosega. Nibardo's concern for the Tuiolosega family and his love for Lima Lama was steadfast.

Most of my martial arts life was spent as Tino close friend and student. In fact, I developed a sincere affection for the Tuiolosega family. It was because of this deep personal feeling that I bowed out as Executive Technical Director. Why? I believed that my involvement might keep the father and son relationship from growing through Lima Lama. Nibardo also saw what lay ahead and graciously stepped aside. As Tino's son, Rudy assumed his rightful place at the top of the Lima Lama hierarchy. And just as I expected, Nibardo continued to teach Tino's Lima Lama and proudly display the organization's emblem. As one of the art's most-ardent supporters, he continues to teach and spread the Lima Lama message in Mexico.

As for my self, I continued to produce my martial arts show after my departure from Lima Lama. My quest for knowledge remains part of my daily life as I continue to pursue martial arts excellence. In 2012, I finally completed my written martial arts documentations thus created my own teaching system and style of self-defense called the A.G. Matrix System. It is a system of three parts, the methodology of teaching (progressive teaching method), the system (beginning, middle, and end) and the style of movements (executions).

# Chapter 35

## A Dear Friend Claire Panini Nelson Tuiolosega

On Dec. 3, 1999, Tino's first wife, Claire, died of a heart attack. She was living in Riverside, CA, with her sister and was experiencing health issues at the time of her death. I saw her a couple of years earlier and she was the picture of health. In 1997 I called and asked if I could do an interview for my martial arts cable television show. I told her I wanted an interview about the early history of Tino, herself and the origins and development of Lima Lama. She agreed we arranged to meet me at Kaipo's Huntington Beach home, which was just a few doors down from her apartment. She was a little nervous at first when she saw the camera. I told her I wanted it to be a conversation between two old friends, rather than just a standard question-and-answer session. That evening, we filmed hours on Tino's early childhood, his Marines service, his time in Hawaii and the history and development of Lima Lama. It was less an interview and more a casual meeting between two old acquaintances. We talked, laughed, joked and enjoyed ourselves like two friends who haven't seen each other in years. She was a classy woman who loved her family and friends.

A year later, I received a call from my friend Don (Tino's friend and student). He told me Claire was in the hospital and according to her doctor, only had a few weeks to live. Her relatives in Hawaii were informed of her condition and flew to California to pay their last respects. I prayed for my good friend Claire. As I prayed for her, the Lord told me I should visit her. I was hesitant at first, but something inside told me to go see Claire.

So I decided to go that day and pray for a healing. When I arrived at the hospital, I went upstairs to her room and from the door I saw her alone asleep. She appeared pale and very sick. I called her name, but she wouldn't answer. I stood next to her bed, held her hand and asked the Lord to heal her body and make her well. I did as I was told. A feeling of deep relief and gladness welled up inside me. I was obedient and pleased with myself. After I prayed, I put her hand down and left the hospital. A day later, Don told me Claire had left the hospital and was well enough to go home. I knew God had healed her.

Six months later, Cookie called and told me her mom wanted to see me. When I arrived Cookie and her mom were at poolside watching the kids swim. After saying hello to her and the grandchildren, Cookie said,

*"Thank you for praying for my mom."*

She then related a story about what her mom said happened after my visit to the hospital.

I sat next to Claire. She also thanked me. I said, *"For what?"*

*"For praying for me at the hospital,"* she answered. *"Al, the day you came to see me, the strangest thing happened to me after you prayed for me. My body got really hot and after you left, I got out of bed, got dressed and left the hospital. Yah really Al, it happened just like that. Thank you for praying for me."* She replied.

*"You are welcome."* I said.

She recalled that all her relatives had flown in from Hawaii to see her one last time.

*"But you see Al, I'm fine now. I'm not going to die like what the doctors had said."*

She smiled and held my hand for a few seconds. We visited a little while longer and then I left. She died a year later. The Lord had given her one more year to enjoy her family, life and friends. Here was her obituary:

*Claire P.N. Tuiolosega, age 66, of Riverside, Calif., a retired licensed vocational nurse, died Dec. 3. 1999. She was born 1933 in Honolulu. She is survived by daughters Arlette Kaleopa and Kimberlee Tuiolosega; sons Nelson, Rudolph, Eric, Myron and Norman; brother Rudolph Nelson, Jr.; sister Harriet M. McCabe, 18 grandchildren and six great-grandchildren. Services: 9 a.m. Thursday at Waianae Boat Harbor. Scattering of ashes: Pokai Bay. Casual attire.*

## Tino's Passing

After spending years on the road doing seminars around the world, Tino, Adele and Rudy returned to California for a well-deserved rest.

On March 22, 2011, Tino died from heart failure with his family by his side. He was 79. He is survived by his wife of 32 years, Adele Tuiolosega Radicchi and his children, Arlette "Cookie" Kaleopa, Nelson Tuiolosega, Rudolph Tuiolosega, Eric Tuiolosega, Myron Tuiolosega, Kaipo Tuiolosega, Kimberlee Tuiolosega, Michael Wilson, Sapoaluga Toki, Ilina Suliafu, Joseph Tuiolosega-Radicchi, their beloved spouses, and a legacy of 37 grandchildren and 30 great-grandchildren. He is also survived by his sisters Maave Jamias, Toeaga Gansit, Malologa Balete, Flowerpot Salas, Tolise Palaita, Ulata Tanya Saui'a, Gafa Poumele, Taumaloto Tuiolosega and beloved brother, Trevor Tuiolosega, as well as many other loving family members and relatives including his mother-in-law Nuni Radicchi, who lovingly called him Lui, during the early days in Santa Cruz.

The funeral service was held on Friday, April 1, 2011, at Benito and Azzaro Pacific Gardens Chapel in Santa Cruz.

Unfortunately, I had a horrible case of influenza and was unable to attend the service. To this day I regret not attending the service. But I'm sure he knows in my heart I miss him.

# GM Tino In Samoa RIP

# Chapter 36
## Back at the Stadium

*The Master is just about to go on. He has one last reflection.*

*I'm here ready to demonstrate in front of over 400 black belts from the Mexican Lima Lama Federation, the biggest Lima Lama organization in the world. It's amazing what Tino accomplished with his Lima Lama. Here I am wearing Tino's Lima Lama patch on one side and my own Matrix system patch on the other side. I think Tino would be proud.*

*The Master stands and begins his walk toward the arena entrance. He can now see the packed house of spectators and Black Belt practitioners. The audience stands and applauds as he walks toward the center of the arena. His assistant joins him and the demonstration begins.*

**Standing GM Al Garza (Matrix System) with his students to his right**

*End of the Beginning Story*

## Conclusion

After Tino's passing, Lima Lama was once again without a leader. The affiliated organizations that had pledged their support when the Grandmaster was alive seized the opportunity go out on their own. They quickly formed separate groups and had no trouble appointing themselves Grandmasters of their specific styles.

Like so many arts before them—the most recent being Ed Parker's Kenpo, Bruce Lee's Jeet Kune Do or Karate's Robert Trias—students who would never have thought of abandoning their teachers when they were alive, had no trouble leaving them behind after they were gone. No one is faulting first- and second-generation students for following their own martial arts path. After all, any good teacher will encourage freethinking and experimentation. He (or she) hopes the student will find their own way. However, all that is asked is for a student to remember his roots, to pay homage to the vehicle that sent him on his way.

Thanks to Tino's dedication, Lima Lama can still be found throughout the world. Sadly, the organizations and Grandmasters who owe their very existence and livelihood to this martial arts giant have refused to repay the favor. The man that breathed life into a fighting style should be remembered for his sacrifices, not forgotten by those closest to him.

Each Lima Lama practitioner has to remember that we are all part of the whole no matter what name we carry or who our teacher is. We are all Lima Lama. Unity is strength, divided we fall.

**BEGINNING OF TIME LINE:**

*Early 1920*—Tino's father, High Chief, Tuumamao Tuiolosega and mother Sapo Alugo, originally from the Island of Olosega and Sapsapoaluga Feagaimaleata Poumele Tuiolosega, move to Pago Pago American Samoa.

1930—Tino is born in Pago Pago, American Samoa.

1947—Tino joins the U.S. Marines at the age of 17.

1952—Nineteen-year-old Claire meets boxer Tino Tuiolosega in Hawaii.

1953—Tino and Claire marry and have their first child in 1954. Another is child welcomed in 1955 and a third in 1956. They add four more children in 1958, 1960, 1961 and 1962, respectively.

1955—Tino receives an honorable discharge from the Marine Corps. He then enrolls as a student at the University of Hawaii, while moonlighting as a Hawaiian Knife and Fire dancer.

1956—Tino leaves his wife and children in Pago Pago while searching for work in California. In California, Tino resides at his cousin's house in the city of Maywood, near Los Angeles. He finds employment at a manufacturing company.

1956—Claire returns to California, but Tino's Samoan background makes it difficult for them to find an apartment. Claire comes to the rescue and the pair finds a place to live.

1956—After being promoted to supervisor, the couple moves to San Gabriel, California.

1956—Tino and Claire see an advertisement for Kenpo Karate being taught by Ed Parker in Pasadena, CA. By coincidence, Parker is the son of the minister that married Tino and Claire in Hawaii.

1963—Tino meets Ed Parker and quickly becomes his student. Parker, who will someday be known as the "Father of American Karate," is one of five students of the legendary William Kwai Sun Chow who brought Kenpo Karate derivatives from Hawaii. Parker sees something special in his young student and gives him the task of training the advanced Black Belt classes, even though he is just a brown belt. In time, becomes Ed Parker's "right-hand man".

1964—Tino's non-stop ambition takes him across town to the studio of Grandmaster Ark Wong, one of the best and most-influential Chinese martial arts masters in America.

1964—Ark Wong teaches "Sil Lum Pai", the five animals of Shaolin. The animals are Dragon, Tiger, Snake, Leopard and Crane. He also teaches Tai Chi Chuan, five-element fist, Hop Gar Lama and 18 traditional weapons of the Shaolin Temple.

1965—Tino Tuiolosega continues his second year with grandmaster Ed Parker and studies with Grandmaster Ark Wong.

1965—Albert Garza trains in Karate with Mr. Dan Guzman and meets Sal Esquivel and Richard Nunez at Cleveland House Gymnasium in East Los Angeles.

1965—Tino begins organizing and documenting the art of Lima Lama. He also starts designing a special Lima Lama patch.

1965—After training in Karate at Dan Guzman's School, Albert Garza meets Tino Tuiolosega and Tiny Lefiti. It is an event that changes Albert Garza's direction in life. Tino shares the concepts behind Lima Lama and the techniques that make the art special. Tiny relates that he has a Lima Lama and Kung-Fu School in Huntington Park. His business partner is Ralph Shun.

1965—The first Lima Lama board is created
Tino Tuiolosega names five students to his first Lima Lama organization Board of Directors. They are: Tiny Lefiti,

Richard Nunez, Sal Esquivel, John Louis and Solomon Kaihewalu.

1965--- Al Garza follows GM Tino visits to Richard Nunez school and learns from GM Tino.

1966—At the same time, one of Albert Garza's first teachers, Dan Guzman, visits Ed Parker's home to receive private Karate lessons. It is there that he meets Bruce Lee. A gentleman riding a motorcycle parks in front of Dan Guzman's School during a Karate class. His student, Albert Garza, becomes curious, walks to the window, turns around and announces to his classmates in a raised voice: "It's Bruce Lee!"

1966-Albert Garza becomes a student of Tiny Lefiti, Ralph Shun and Tino's student. Tiny trains in Lima Lama with Tino and in Kung-Fu with Ralph Shun, who receives formal instruction from Grandmaster Ark Wong.

1967-1968—Tino is named "Grandmaster" for his proficiency in the Five Animals of Shaolin and of the Five Chinese Families styles of Kung-Fu. This marks the first time a non-Chinese earns distinguished   recognition from Chinese Kung-Fu Grandmasters.

1968—At Tino's home in Diamond Bar, Tiny Lefiti learns Lima
Lama under Tino, while Albert Garza observes the instruction
and training. After a year and half of intense training Tino,
Tiny Lefiti and Ralph Shun promote Albert Garza to the rank
of Black Belt in Lima Lama, Kung-Fu: Five Animal Style and
the Mok Ga Style. Also promoted to Black Belt in the same
styles is Gary Knutsen. Those promotions constitute the first
Black Belts handed out at the Huntington Park school.

1968—A young Albert Garza becomes the official student of
Grandmaster Tino Tuiolosega after receiving private instruction
at the Grandmaster's home two-to-three times per week. Tino
later shows his Ancestry book to Al Garza.

1968—In Diamond Bar, Al Garza becomes aware of the tough-as-
nails training session Tino conducts with his first students using
the application of "Dim Mok".

1968—Albert Garza asks Tino to describe the differences between
the Master Kung-Fu forms and the commercial Kung-Fu forms.
Tino smiles and says, "Watch, I'll do the Tiger form so you can
see the differences." Tino's movements are precise, sharp, quick
and powerful.

1968—Tino and Bruce Lee have been friends from their days at Ed Parker's school. Tino invites Bruce to his Luau as his special guest and requests a demonstration of Bruce's Jeet Kune Do fighting system. Bruce Lee accepts the invitation to the Hawaiian Luau celebration and is present at the Lua festivities in the city of San Gabriel.

1968—Bruce Lee sits with Tino Tuiolosega and Ed Parker in the first row at the San Gabriel Auditorium during at the Luau festivities. Bruce Lee also delights the Luau crowd with an extraordinary demonstration.

1968—Tino's demonstration with his students at the San Gabriel Luau is impressive and shows how much force can be generated.

1968—While studying video production in college, Albert Garza begins to film Tino's Lima Lama demonstrations.

1968—Albert Garza meets Rigo Lopez at Tino's residence in Diamond Bar.

1969—An unforgettable Lima Lama exhibition is held at the Bull Fighting Ring arena "Plaza de Toros" in Tijuana, Mexico.

1969—Alberto Garza joins the United States Coast Guard.

1971—Tino's suffers his first heart attack. After two weeks Tino shows signs of improvement, but he remains in serious condition and requires care.

1971—During his stay in the hospital, Tino teaches his student, Albert, the finger sets. Upon finishing, Tino warns Albert not to reveal these techniques to anyone, because they are derived from "Dim Mok," or the Chinese "touch of death".

1971—Albert Garza returns a week later and Tino announces: "Guess who called me last night?" The answer: Elvis Presley.

1971—Rigo Lopez is the first student in Mexico to be awarded a Black Belt in Lima Lama under Tino Tuiolosega.

1971—Rigo Lopez opens a Lima Lama School in Tijuana, Mexico. His students later spread Lima Lama throughout the world

1971— Albert Garza completes his military service and leaves the U.S. Coast Guard. He gets married, moves to Alhambra, CA., and continues his study of Lima Lama with his teacher, Tino.

1971—Albert Garza opens his first commercial Lima Lama School in San Gabriel, CA.

1972—Tino opens his first commercial Lima Lama School in Westminster, CA. His business partner is Futi Seamanu, a Black Belt under Tiny Lefiti.

1973—In February, Tiny Lefiti dies of a heart attack at the age of 43.

1974—Albert Garza promotes his first Lima Lama students—Rudy Ramirez and Robert Tygenhoff—to Black Belt.

1975—Tino is Albert Garza's special guest on his television show.

1978-79—Tino Tuiolosega retires and travels to a foreign country, where he disappears from Lima Lama for 13 years.

1983—Tino is living in Santa Cruz with his wife, Adele, and son, Joey and teaching Kenposilama.

In 1984, long-time friend and one of Garza's first student Hector Castaneda, is promoted to Black Belt.

1989-1990—Tino returns to Lima Lama as the Grandmaster. Albert Garza and his son, Albert Garza II, begin a search for Tino in Mexico City.

1993—It's Tino's 60 birthday and he celebrates with his students in Santa Cruz, CA. Albert Garza and his son join friends and family for the celebration at the Kenposilama School in Santa Cruz.

1993—Albert Garza films Santa Cruz students Bill, Raphael, Dio and Clara demonstrating Kenposilama basic fundamentals.

1993—Practitioners from Spain visit Tino in Santa Cruz, CA., for the second time and remain for six months. The students from Spain are: Carlos Becerra, Juan F. Freire Fernandez, Alfonso Guerrero, Felipe Cachón, and Jose Gómez.

1994—Tino schedules a trip to Spain.

1994—Upon arriving in Los Angeles after visiting Tino in Santa Cruz, Albert Garza receives a call from Adele that Tino has suffered a heart attack and stroke.

1994—Albert Garza visits Tino in Santa Cruz.
Before leaving to Spain, Albert Garza visits Tino numerous times in Santa Cruz.

1995—Albert Garza accompanies Tino and his family to Spain were he films the trip.

1995—The plane trip from Los Angeles to Madrid takes 14 hours. They arrive tired but excited at the thought of sharing Lima Lama with the Spaniards.

1995—Santa Cruz student Raphael is given the honor of conducting Lima Lama seminars under the supervision of Grandmaster Tino. Tino demonstrates, but the stroke has left him with limited motion in his hands and feet.

1995—Tino is the Guest of Honor at the Barcelona Lima Lama Tournament. Once again, Tino demonstrates with Raphael. Afterward, Raphael and Joey demonstrate.

1995—Albert Garza films the tour and airs the footage on his martial arts television show.

1996—A year after the trip to Spain, Albert Garza receives an invitation from Tino for another trip, this time to American Samoa, Tutuila (Pago Pago). Albert meets Tino's Mom, adopted brothers and sisters. Albert also films the events and shows the images on his television program, "The World of Martial Arts."

1996—Al Garza travels with Tino and his family to Cancun, Mexico.

1996—In Cancun, Nibardo Sanchez is promoted to 8$^{th}$-degree Lima Lama Black Belt by Tino. Sanchez studied from Lima Lama teacher Rigo Lopez.

1997—The interaction between Al Garza and Nibardo Sanchez in California and during the Cancun trips leads to a lifelong friendship.

1997—Albert Garza reveals the Lima Lama curriculum he has developed as a system to Nibardo. Nibardo reports that the curriculum is well-organized and structured.

1998—In California, Tino Tuiolosega holds a meeting attended by his wife, Nibardo Sanchez and Albert Garza. Albert formally presents his curriculum to the group.

1999—Three years after the Cancun trip, Grandmaster and founder, Tino Tuiolosega, promotes his friend and student Nibardo Sanchez to the rank of 9th-degree Black Belt at one of the most-important Black Belt promotion events in Lima Lama history. The event is held at the Double Tree Hotel in Orange County, CA.

1999—Also present at that Black Belt promotion event is Albert Garza, who is charged with filming the notable occasion. Unexpectedly, Tino calls Albert Garza to the front of the room and promotes Albert Garza to the rank of $8^{th}$-degree Black Belt.

1999—Rudy Tuiolosega expresses his interest in teaching Lima Lama and joining the Lima Lama organization. The group welcomes him with open arms.

1999—Claire, Tino's first wife, dies of a heart attack.

1999—Rudy Tuiolosega is promoted to $10^{th}$-degree Black Belt in Lima Lama by his father, Tino.

1999— Nibardo Sanchez leaves the position of director of Tino's organization and returns to Mexico. Nibardo does this as a sign of respect for Tino, as well as Tino's son, Rudy.

1999—Al Garza retires from the Lima Lama Organization and forms his own system and teaching methodology called the A.G. Matrix System.

1999—Nibardo Sanchez continues to demonstrate his love and respect for Tino Tuiolosega and his family, as well as his devotion to Lima Lama in Mexico.

2000—One of the largest martial arts organizations in Mexico, the Federation of Mexico of Lima Lama, organizes the first Black Belt Tournament in Mexico City.

2000—Albert Garza is now the Matrix Founder and Grandmaster of his own system and promotes to Black Belt in A.G. Matrix System and Lima Lama, Bill Rosary, Tom Chan and Frank Juarez.

Matrix's First Master Class

2000—Albert Garza begins teaching his Master Class with renown Grandmasters, masters, and high-ranking Black Belts, including Kung-Fu GM Eric Lee; Kung-Fu GM Carl Totton, also a 7th-degree Black Belt under Ed Parker; Kung-Fu Master Tom Chan, who studied in GM Ark Wong's Kung-Fu system and is a Black Belt in Karate; Master Wilson Quan, who studied under Ark Wong and Tiny Lefiti and is a Black Belt in Judo; Bill Rosary, a Black Belt in Lima Lama and now a Grandmaster in Tai Chi system; Frank Juarez, a Black Belt in Lima Lama; Nibardo Sanchez, a 9th degree in Lima Lama; GM Doug Wong and GM Carrie Wong.

2013—The Matrix System is complete with Black Belt requirements from white belt to 10th degree, Grandmaster level. All requirements are documented.

2013—Albert Garza promotes the first A.G. Matrix System intermediate Black Belt levels ($2^{nd}$- and $3^{rd}$-degree Black Belt) to Phil Sanchez, Stan Wong, Frank Juarez, and Xavier Duggan. Also promoted in the Lima Lama System is Aram Sanchez.

2013—Al Garza promotes Phil Sanchez, Stan Wong, Frank Juarez, Xavier Duggan and Nibardo Aram Sanchez to $5^{th}$-degree Black Belt in the Lima Lama system.

2014—The first A.G. Matrix System Organization is formed.

## Associate Teachers in A.G. Matrix Combative System

**Xavier Duggan – Aram Sanchez- GM Al Garza-
Frank Juarez- Phil Sanchez – Stan Wong**

**A.G. Matrix Board Advisor and lifetime practitioner A. Falcon. With GM Al Garza**

**Al Garza's first Black Belts**

**Al Garza II – A. Falcon - GM Al Garza – Bill Rosary - Tom Chan**

# Al Garza's Picture Time Line

**Grand Master Tino with Sal Esquivel demonstrating Lima Lama**

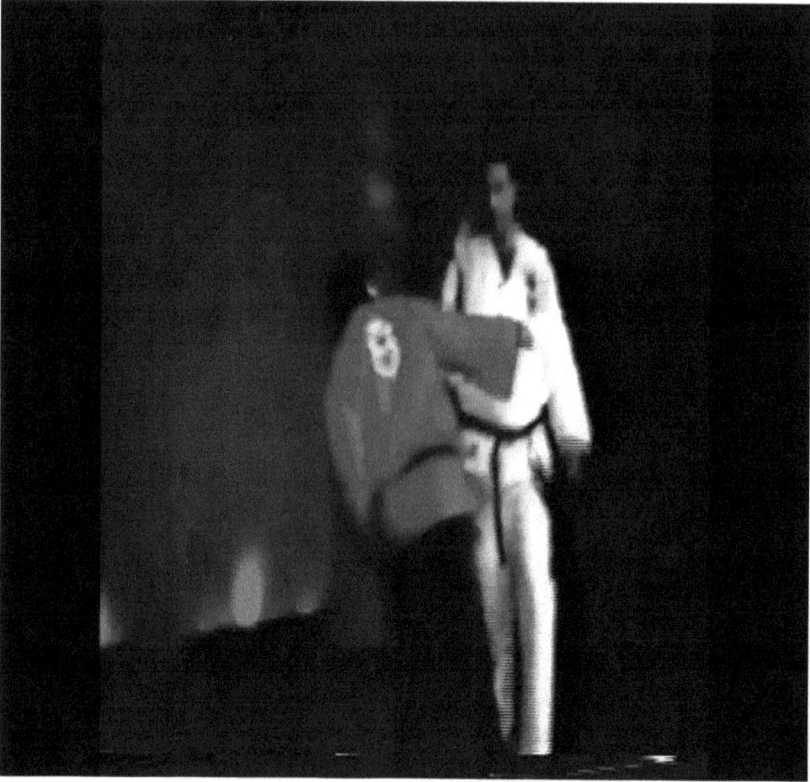

Al Garza receiving his First Degree Black Belt in Lima Lama and Kung-Fu .

My Kung-fu teacher Ralph Shun with Tiny Lefiti with GM Ark Wong

**Party with family 1968**

**Tiny with wife Alice, Al Garza, Mom Rebecca Garza, Tino Dad Alfred Garza, Claire, and Tiny's sister with kids.**

**Al Garza and GM Tino Tuiolosega**

**Below Tino, Vernon Wells and Al Garza**

**The World Of Martial Arts Cable Show in 1975**

# From the World Of Martial Arts

**Grand Master Tino Tuiolosega 1975**

# GM Tiny Lefiti 1968 Pictures

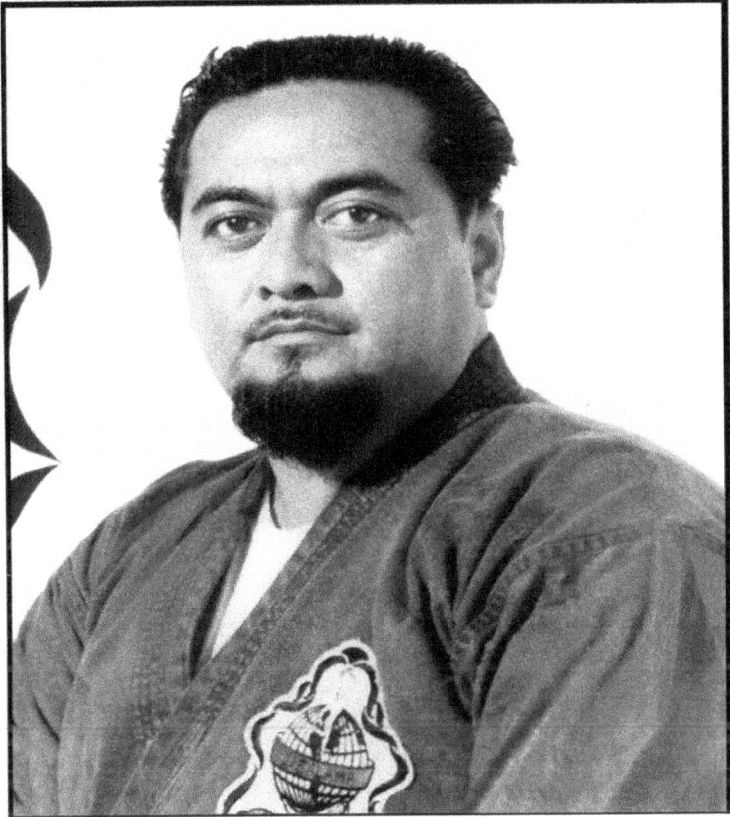

# GM Richard Nunez 1993

## GM Sal Esquivel 1993

**GM John Louis 1967**

## GM Solomon Kaihewalu 1993

## Al Garza II And GM Al Garza Sr.

## GM Rigo Lopez  1993

**GM Al Garza with Long time friend and Lima Lama Practitionor, Don Lombardo - Attorney At Law 2014**

# Claire and Tino Tuiolosega

**Buzzy  Eric  Rudy Cookie  Kim  1969**

# Kaipo  Rudy Myron

# Taumaloto and Family

Al Garza   GM Tino
Dad and Tino
Mom And Al Garza

Al Garza  GM Tiny Lefitie
Fugi, Al Garza  GM Richard Nunez
Al Garza   Tino Tuiolosega

1969 Al Garza Going to Coast Guard Party

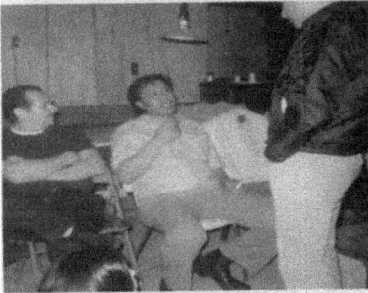

# Al Garza's 1975
## World Of Martial Arts TV Cable
## Program

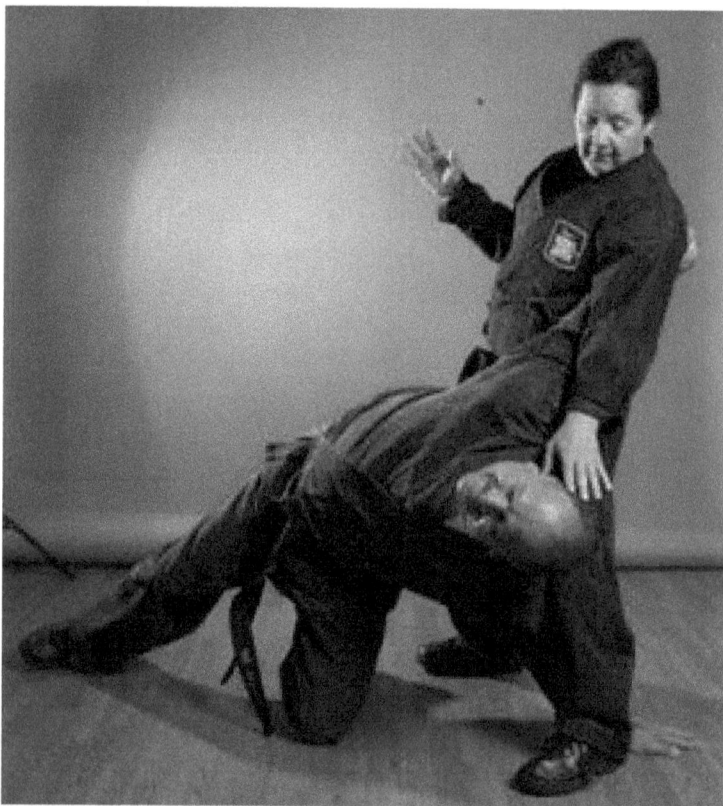

# DVD Collection Lima Lama From Al Garza's World Of Martial Arts Videoed in 1974 and 1975

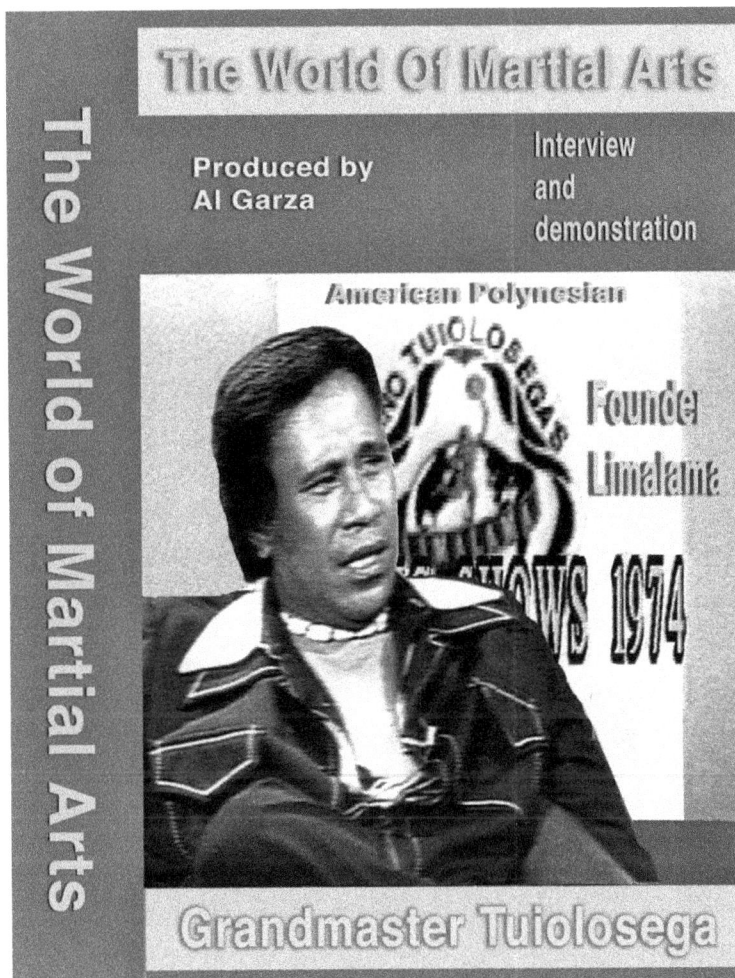

**Al Garza Producer**
**The World Of Martial Arts TV Program**
**GM  Tino Tuiolosega  Co-Host Vernon Wells  Host Al Garza**

# Technique by GM Tino Tuiolosega

1

2

3

4

5

6

**GM Ed Parker 1975**
**Produced By Al Garza – Co-Host Vernon Wells**

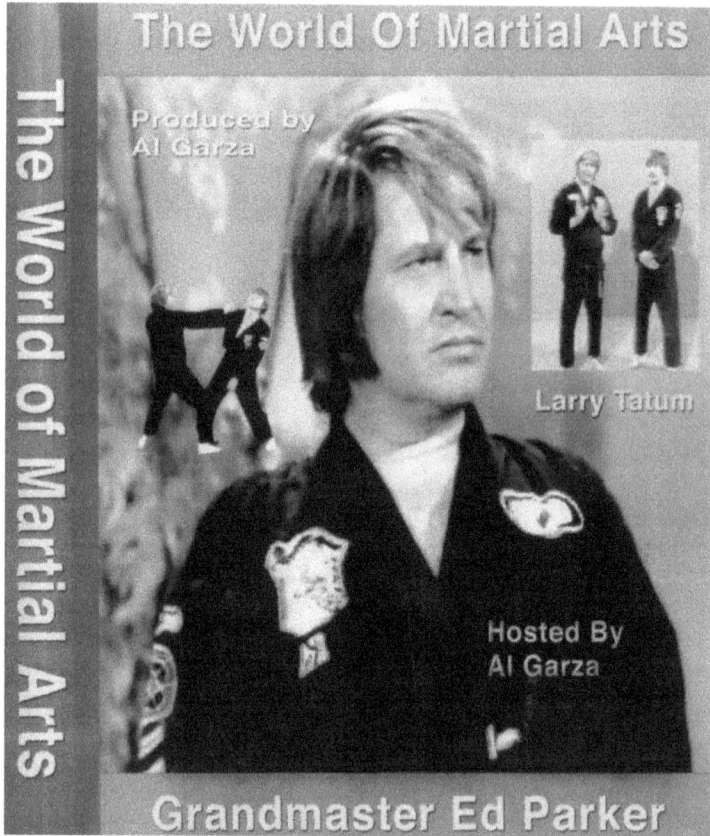

# GM Ed Parker And Al Garza In World Of Martial Arts Studio

## Pictures Inside WMA Studio 1975

# 1991 Santa Cruz School KenpoSilama

**Bill – Myron- Rudy – Ralph –Dio**

## GM Tino With Joey and Albert II

## Grandmaster Tino And Grandson

# GM Tino And Al Garza In Spain 1995

## Madrid -Toledo And Barcelona

Juan F. Fernandez, Jose Gomez, Alfonso Guerrero

**Students, Alfonso Guerrero, Joey, GM Tino, Jose Gomez, Rafael Granados, Al Garza and Carlos Becerra.**

# GM Tino and Adele

## Toledo Spain

# Al Garza And Joey Tuiolosega In Toledo Spain

# Demonstration By GM Tino In Spain

## Bercelona Spain

# Our travel to the Hawaiian Islands
## Lanai – Oahu - Kauai

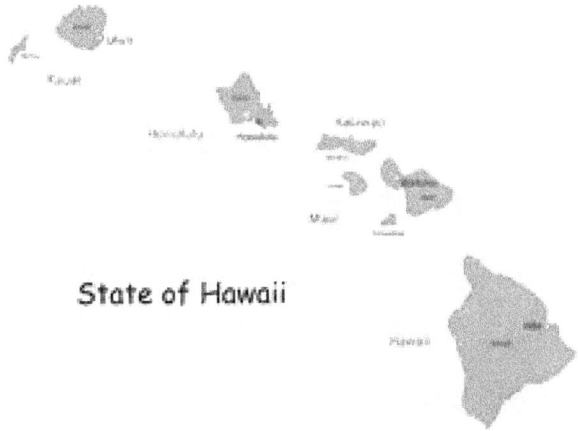

State of Hawaii

**Having a great time in Hawaii**

Joey Tuiolosega  GM Tino  Adele  Un-known  Al Garza

**GM Tino Teaching A Seminar in Hawaii 1996**

# Kauai Hawaii

## Sleeping Giant

**GM Tino   Adele  GM Doug Mc Leod**

**GM Teaching In Kauai Hawaii**

**Al Garza in Kauai Filming For The World Of Martial Arts Show**

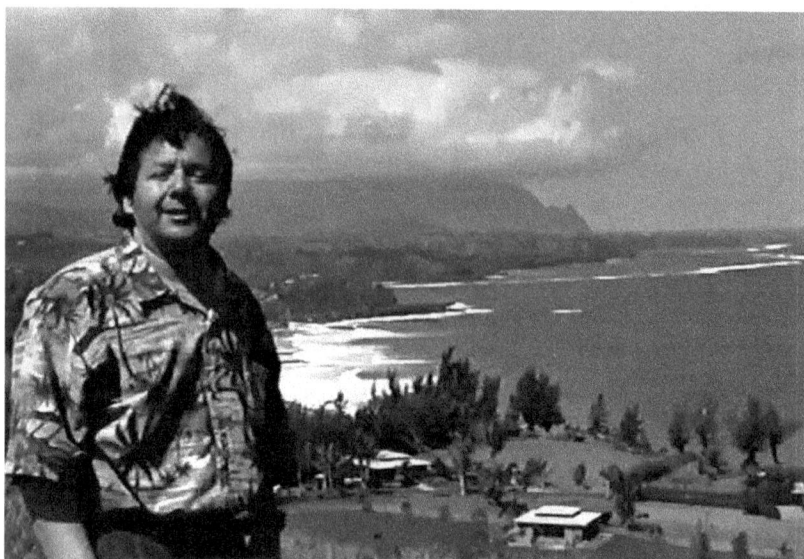

# Our Trip To American Samoa 1996

## Village In Tutuila

# American Samoa  Pago Pago

## Al Garza, Joey, GM Tino And Son Eric Tuiolosega

## Adele, Joey, Trevor Tuiolosega And GM Tino

# Downtown In Pago Pago

**School Kids Taking A Break**

**Joey Tuiolosega And Al Garza**

# GM Tino And His Mom Saposapoaluga Feagaimaleata Poumele Tuiolosega

# Cancun the Riveria of Mexico

**Nibardo Sanchez  GM Tino  Guide  Adele And Yvette Sanchez**

**Nibardo Sanchez  Al Garza  GM Tino Tuiolosega**

## GM Tino Demonstrating A Lima Lama Technique

Dave Coronel  Joey  GM Tino  Nibardo Sanchez  Adele –
Yvette Sanchez

# Founder Lima Lama Grand Master Tino Tuiolosega

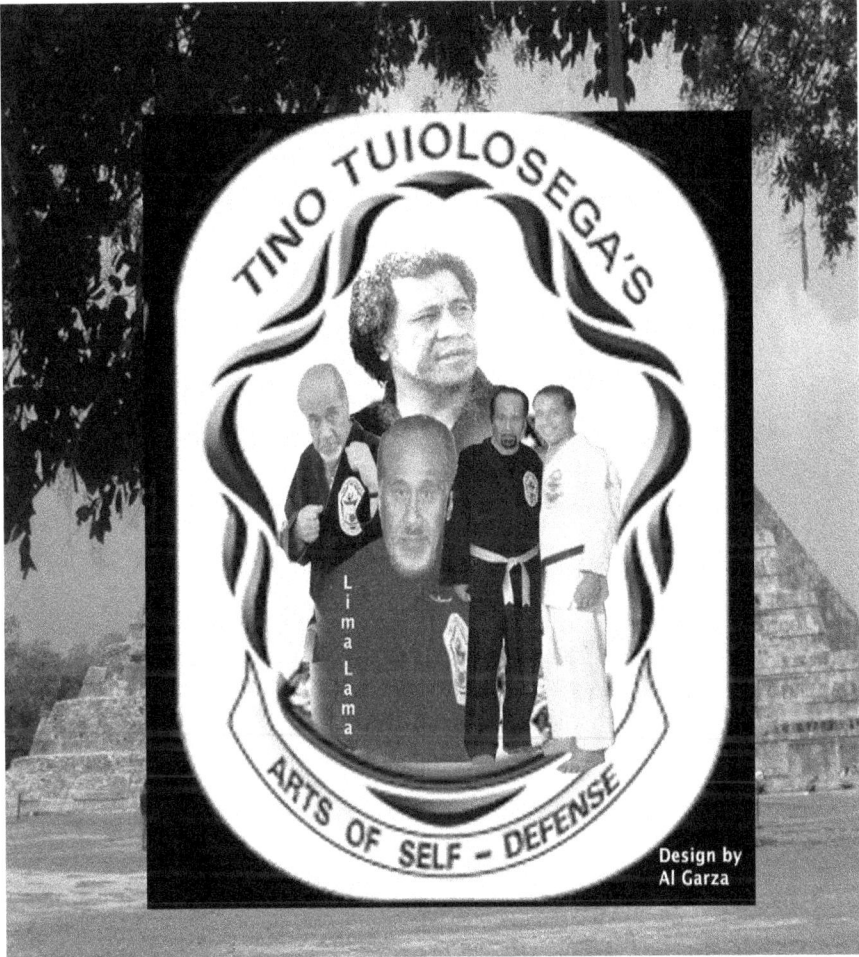

# Rest in Peace My Teacher And Friend

**GM Tino And Author  Al Garza**

**My Story, Memories of A Marital Art Grand Master**

## Author's Biography

Al Garza

57 years in Martial Arts

8th degree in Lima Lama

Founder and creator of A.G. Matrix System and A.G. Combative System

Creator of the self-defense Progressive Teaching Method

Master Instructor in Five Animals Kung-fu system

Master Instructor of Master Class in Los Angeles

Taught self-defense at Cal State Pomona University as a staff teacher

Producer and creator of "The World Of Martial Arts" Cable TV show

Master Teacher of high-ranking martial artist from various systems Al Garza has been interviewed many times in Inside Kung-fu magazine

Producer of Matrix training videos

Specializing in Women's self-defense programs

Educated in Boxing, Judo, Karate, Kung-fu, Ground movements, Lima Lama and Grand Master and Founder of A.G. Matrix systems.

www.ingramcontent.com/pod-product-compliance
Lightning Source LLC
Chambersburg PA
CBHW060016100426
42740CB00010B/1501